Claude Quillet

Callipædiæ

Or, an art how to have handsome children

Claude Quillet

Callipædiæ
Or, an art how to have handsome children

ISBN/EAN: 9783337386184

Printed in Europe, USA, Canada, Australia, Japan

Cover: Foto ©Lupo / pixelio.de

More available books at **www.hansebooks.com**

CALLIPÆDIÆ.

OR,

AN ART

HOW TO HAVE HANDSOME

CHILDREN:

WRITTEN IN LATIN

BY THE

ABBOT CLAUDE QUILLET.

Now done into English Verse
by several hands.

[Fac-Simile of London Editions of 1708-10.]

PHILADELPHIA:
PRINTED FOR THE
AMERICAN ANTIQUARIAN PUBLISHING COMPANY.
1872.

HISTORY OF THE BOOK,
AND ITS AUTHOR.

CLAUDE QUILLET, an ingenious French writer of Latin Poetry, born at Chinon in Tourine, 1602, died 1661. First Edition of the Callipædiæ printed at *Leyden*, 1655, 4to, under title of *Calvidii Leti Callipædia, seu Pulchræ Prolis habendæ Ratione*. Second Edition, *Paris*, 1656, with many additions, and Quillet's proper name to it.

Latin imprint (Gr. Pap. 46 f.),   London, 1708, 8vo.
  " "   Paris, 1709, 8vo.

"There exist several versions '*In English verse by several hands*,'" *London*, 1710, 1712 and 1715. By Will. Oldisworth, *London*, 1719, in 8vo. By N. Rowe, *London*, 1720, 1733, 1760, in 8vo.

There is also an imitation under the following title: "The Joys of Hymen or, the Conjugal Directory; a Poem in three Books." *London*, 1768, in 8vo.

Translated into French by Lancelin de Laval, with Latin Text. *Paris, Bastien*, 1774, in 8vo.

Another French translation by J. M. Caillau, *Bordeaux, Pinard (An VII.)*, 1799, in 12mo.

Another translation, by Montenault d'Egly, with Latin text. *Paris*, 1749, 8vo, (17 f. *de Cotte* 37 f. 50 c. *Caillard*).

CALLIPÆDIÆ.

BOOK I.

 SING the pleasures of the Nuptial Bed,
And the fair Product of the Genial Seed,
What Skies, propitious to the dear Embrace,
Imprint their Brightness on a beauteous Face;
How, in one happy Object, we may find
A charming Body with a lovely Mind;
How the glad Parents, when the Boy is Born,
With shining Virtues may his Soul adorn.
 Ye Goddesses, who move and melt the Heart,
Ye Graces, to the Muse your Gifts impart;
And Thou, their Queen, who on th' *Idalian* Hill
With Rapture didst the *Phrygian* Shepherd fill,
Whose naked Beauties blest his greedy Eyes,
And with full Justice gain'd the Golden Prize;

CALLIPÆDIÆ.

Inspire my Song, and teach me to rehearse
The Cause, the Pow'r of Love, in grateful Verse.
Good wives, perhaps, will to my Rules attend,
By tender Husbands taught, who can't offend;
She'll listen to my Lays, whose pious Pray'r
Pleads, that the promis'd Issue may be fair.
Let Men no more the Nuptial Fruit despise,
Nor view the crooked Babe with loathsome Eyes.
No more let *Hymeneal* Joys be curst, .
Nor Forms, ill Shap'd, with hated care be Nurst.

You, who for Beauteous Sons and Daughters pray,
My Precepts hear, and what you hear, obey.
And if the Poet's Lessons you allow,
Crown, in return, with Myrtle Wreaths his Brow.
But what is Beauty let us first Inquire,
For diff'rent Charms create the same Desire.
In what do's the Supream Perfection lye,
Or in the Lilly Look, or sparkling Eye?
The balmy Lip, the slender Shape, or Hair,
A finish'd Form, or an engaging Air?
For Lovers are in doubt, and this to me
Is Shocking, which perhaps is Grace to thee.
Fair *Amaryllis* has her Vot'ries here,
And swarthy *Chloris* her Admirers there.
Thee *Sylvia's* Golden Tresses charm, and thou,
Oh *Thyrsis*, doat'st on *Daphne's* sooty Brow:

CALLIPÆDIÆ.

Thou hat'st the Sandy Lock; one loves to play
With the kind Nymph whose killing Eyes are Grey:
The Coal-black Eye another Lover fires,
This a Lean Maid, a Fleshy that desires.
Such Heresie's in Love's Religion spread,
And blindly each alike by Lust is led.
  Nor is the various Gust of Beauty new;
Of old, each Nation lik'd a different Hue.
Thus the fair Face did *Æthiopians* fright,
And Fiends were by their Fancy painted white.
Thus the high Nose, and Arch'd, the *Persians* pleas'd
Of old, and all the Dwellers of the *East*.
Fam'd for this Form, was he, who held the Reins
Of Rule, o'er *Asia's* vast united Plains,
And *Lydia's* Wealthy Monarch led in Chains.
Pleasure the *Gauls* in fair Complexions took,
In long curl'd Locks, and in an open Look.
The Boaster *Spaniard*, whom the setting Sun
Fills with black Blood, and dies a dusky Dun,
Who with big words the Heav'n that burns him braves,
And with vain Threats a double World Enslaves,
Thinks ev'ry Beauty, ev'ry Grace, is seen
In his lank Hair, and his Majestick Mien.
Dutch dangling Arms are scorn'd by him and scoft,
And *Britains* he despises as too soft.

CALLIPÆDIÆ.

Whence rises this Debate, in things so clear?
Whence does this Fair, and that Deform'd appear?
Say, Muse, What hidden Cause divides Mankind?
Their Fancy why so various, and so blind?
To the Spring trace this Error, and declare
Why all are not agreed, that one is Fair.

As yet the World its Purity maintain'd,
And spotless Innocence and Beauty reign'd.
As yet the Mettal was without Allay,
Nor had the Iron made its Impious Way.
Bright was the Golden Day, the Sky serene,
Nor Cloud was in the Air, nor Vapour seen.
Pure was the *Æther*, and no filthy Fogs
From stagnant Waters rose, and stinking Bogs.
Thou *Phœbus*, Ruler of the Realms of Light,
No Veil hadst known to intercept the Sight.
The Moon, when She thy Radiant Paths pursu'd,
Nor Mist Nocturnal met, nor dreary Cloud.
No Weeds were in the Field, nor Insects found,
Nor the sharp Share had vext the Fruitful Ground.
The Grove, the Greens, Spontaneous Products bear,
And Od'rous Sweets perfume the Balmy Air.
Fair was the Form of Nature, fresh her Face,
No Beauty had she lost as yet, no Grace.
As bright the Chrystal Sky, and *Æther* clear,
So Man was in this Golden Age sincere.

CALLIPÆDIÆ.

From the Sire's Steps the Son did never stray,
Nor wander in a new forbidden Way.
One Worship to the Deathless Gods was paid,
Nor Lust the World, nor lewd Ambition sway'd.
Nor Piety alone adorn'd Mankind,
His Body was as Beauteous as his Mind.
His Features regular, his Limbs were clean,
His Colour lively, and his Look serene.
   When Sov'reign *Jove* from High *Olympus* view'd
The Race of Men, and saw their Ways were good;
Let us, he cry'd our Mighty Work to crown,
Join all that's fair, in Heav'n and Earth, in one;
One Nymph of all the various Beauties frame.
The various Beauties at his summons came;
Swifter than Thought they cut the Azure Sky,
And through the Void to form this Wonder fly.
The Chrystalline supply'd the shining Mould,
And *Phœbus* crown'd her Head with Radiant Gold.
The Moon her Front with Silver Glories grac'd,
The Morn the Rose among the Lillies plac'd.
Her Lips with Honey-Sweets kind *Venus* blest,
Then Love assum'd the Work, and fram'd the rest.
The Graces in the sweet Employment join,
Touch o'er each Part, and make the Piece divine.
The Members forming thus a perfect Frame,
Jove filled the Body with a Vital flame.

Pandora, aptly, then he nam'd the Maid,
And thus the Universal Parent said.
Go, lovely Nymph, to whom the Gods gave Birth,
And bless with gracious Looks th' Obedient Earth.
Conspicuous shall thy Form consummate shine,
And Man's poor Beauty be enrich'd by Thine.
Go, while the happy Age from Guilt is free,
Fair Nature fairer shall commence by Thee.
But if the Pleasure of Mankind's thy Care,
If, as thou'rt form'd, thou would'st be ever fair,
The Box I give thee full of fatal Seed,
With a light Finger to unlock, take heed.
Thy Disobedience will for Vengeance call,
And Plagues on Thee, as well as them, will fall.
He said, and through the Air the Virgin flies
Swifter than Stars, that whirl around the Skies.
Nor did she, as th' *Ascræan* Poet dreams,
First bath her self in *Epimethean* Streams;
But manifest, she by the Croud was seen,
A Goddess in her Look, and in her Mien,
With stupid Eyes they on her Beauties gaz'd,
Pleas'd to Excess, and to Excess amaz'd.
Those her bright Robes, and these her Shape admir'd,
And others with her Golden Curls were fir'd.
She darts a thousand Fiery Glances here,
A thousand Spicy Odours scatters there.

CALLIPÆDIÆ.

And what we scarce can dare to sing, tho' long,
The Muse has taught, and *Phœbus* own'd the Song,
Her Starry Brightness she to them convey'd,
And all around her heav'nly Graces shed.
Thus from the *Eastern* Skies the ruddy Morn
Do's, as she rolls, the smiling Fields adorn.
Fair make the Mead, and fresh the Flow'ry Green,
Glad ev'ry Heart, and ev'ry Look serene.
Her blessings she on either Sex bestow'd,
Their Beauty perfect, as their Manners good.
No Vice did either from strict Virtue draw,
And both were fair, while both observ'd the Law.
But when the guiltless Age to Change began,
And devious were the Mind and Ways of Man,
When his whole Race the foul Infection seiz'd,
And Violence and Lust fill'd ev'ry Breast,
Pandora curst whom she before had blest.
She grows corrupt, the more deprav'd they grew,
Pursues the wicked Paths the World pursue.
And, scorning Heav'ns Supream Commands, unlocks,
Profanely Curious, the forbidden Box.
Thence streight a noisom Stench defil'd the Air,
And turn'd to crawling Snakes her curling Hair.
Soon fled the Native Honours of her Face,
Her Eyes their Brightness lost, her Lips their Grace.

CALLIPÆDIÆ.

A Gum obscene her clammy Eye-lids glew,
And baleful Beams attend her vary'd Hue.
A Goddess once, she now a Fiend appears,
Blasts with her Breath, with what she charm'd she scares.
Nor here do's Heav'ns fore-threaten'd Vengeance end,
An army of Diseases thence ascend.
The fatal Seed a thousand Plagues creates,
And man by Reason neither Loves nor Hates.
Hence what is Beauty none agree, for none
E'er center'd all their diff'rent Tasts in one.
Its Nature to the Race of Men has lain
Long hid, and hid it ever will remain:
For who will drive the gloomy Clouds away,
Scatter the darkness, and restore the Day?
Why, *Phœbus*, is this horrid Night our doom?
What Light will guide us thro' the Starless Gloom?
Oh thou, the God of Day, the God of Verse,
New Light, thy Treasure, with new Rays disperse.

O'er the whole World tho' this Infection spread,
Tho' Beauty from Mankind with Virtue fled,
Yet Partial was her flight, she did not strike
The whole with equal Force, nor Hurt alike.
Much the rude Nations near the Frozen Bear,
The Marks of *Jove's* offended Justice wear.

CALLIPÆDIÆ.

The horrid Natives, on whose burning Coast
The *Southern* Ocean's boiling Waves are tost;
Whose filthy Blood in Sable Channels flows,
And frizled Fleeces hide their narrow Brows;
Whose greasie Lips beneath flat Noses swell,
And strong their nauseous Perspirations smell:
By Beauty these abandon'd most were curst,
Tho' bad the fate of all, yet theirs the worst.
Not quite the Goddess left the temp'rate Spheres,
Where friendly Suns enrich the fruitful Years,
Where Heat and Cold their mutual Pow'rs combine,
And kindly Rays with genial Glories shine.
No baleful Blast the Virgins Beauty spoils,
But a gay Sky with gentle Aspect smiles;
Nor biting Frosts, nor parching Heats prevail,
But *Libra* holds aloft an equal Scale.
The various Seasons plenteous Blessings bring,
And the Year wantons with a double Spring.
The Ground untill'd a Golden Harvest yields,
And Flow'rs unbidden Paint the verdant Fields.
Where chilly Winter looks with chearful Face,
Nor kills the tender Plants, nor nips the Grass,
There Beauty reigns, Eternal Health is there,
Mild are the Climates, and the Natives Fair,
But where ill Habits and Hot Tides within
Affect the Form without, and stain the Skin.

CALLIPÆDIÆ.

You therefore, who a pleasant Clime wou'd find,
To florid Health a Friend, to Beauty kind,
Nor to the Torrid Zone, nor Tropicks fly,
And far behind you leave the Polar Sky.
If lovely Nymphs you seek, and comely Swains,
And what in Man of Human Grace remains,
You must not scorch'd *Iberia's* Wilds explore,
They dwell not there, nor on the *Latian* Shoar.
In Inner *Europe* Beauty spreads her Charms,
She follows Fame as the Reward of Arms.
Where fruitful *France* extends her ample Plains,
Beneath a pure and pleasant Sky she reigns.
But chiefly in *Turonian* Fields resides;
Or where the *Loyre* thro' Flow'ry Meadows glides,
And washes, as he flows, the fertile Lands,
And brightens with his Waves the Yellow Sands.
There beauteous Nymphs you view, whose sparkling
    Eyes
Shine like *Pandora's* e'er she left the Skies.
Nor in their Size too short, nor yet too tall,
But streight, and of a midling Stature all.
Nor Gross, nor Meager, for it pleases none
To see the strutting Flesh, or starting Bone.
Clean are their Limbs, erect their Form, and
    bright
Their charming Faces, as the Morning Light.

CALLIPÆDIÆ.

See how their Fronts in shining Arches rise,
How white their Skin, how keen their killing Eyes.
Their Cherry Lips with balmy Odours blest,
Their Iv'ry Neck behold, their Snowy Breast,
But the Chaste Muse forbids to speak the rest.
  Not only in our Nymphs kind Nature shines,
But in our Manly Youth's severer Lines.
The softer Graces those, the stronger these,
As those the Youth, so these the Virgins please.
A sanguine Look adorns the Beardless Male,
And never do's his equal Temper fail.
Nor stain'd his Face, nor is his Colour wan,
But fresh and fair, as when the Race began.
A graceful Shade around his Temples grow,
And thence in Curls adown his Shoulders flow.
Firm are his Joints; a Well-proportion'd Frame
Agrees, and is in ev'ry Part the same.
These Species from our happy Clime proceed,
Thus *Hymen* blesses here the Nuptial Bed.
Far, or from Artick or· Antartick Pole,
Our friendly Stars between the Tropicks roll.
Heav'n in the Mean, by his peculiar Grace,
Assigns between the two Extreams our Place.
  You now, who are dispos'd to learn our Arts,
Imprint this useful Lesson on your Hearts.

CALLIPÆDIÆ.

Not all of either Sex by *Hymen* join'd,
Are always apt, or shou'd encrease their Kind.
Ne'er, when the Body is defil'd, presume
Within the Temple of the God to come,
Who without Horror hears the Fable tell
Of *Pluto's* Rapes, and the Amours of Hell.
What Virgin cou'd a *Polypheme* behold,
And the foul Monster in her Arms enfold.
No *Vulcan* ought a *Venus* to caress,
Nor her fair Breasts with filthy Fingers press.
Such Wretches shou'd provoke no Virgins Fears,
But end in real Flames their Steril Years.
Nor those who have too long delay'd to Wed,
Shou'd taste the Pleasures of the Marriage-bed,
If seiz'd with Impotence, before they prove
The pleasing Combats of Connubial Love.
Nor those whom Gout or racking Stone devour,
Nor such as dread an Epilepsy's Pow'r,
Nor those who're eaten up with Cank'ring Spleen,
Nor such as tickling Ptisicks waste within,
Nor those whose Veins are full of Fev'rish Blood,
Nor when Consumptions drein the Vital Flood;
For if the Generative Seed's defil'd,
The Father's Hurt's transmitted to the Child.
Ill Habits and Diseases thus are nurst
In the weak Frame, and he with Life is curst.

CALLIPÆDIÆ.

How often have I heard such Infants Cries
Rend, with their fruitless Moan, the guiltless Skies.
You then, who covet Hymeneal Joys,
Consider well before you fix your Choice.
And when your Choice is fix'd with equal Care
Of Bliss dishonest, and ill-tim'd, beware,
Who'd stain his Issue that cou'd have it fair?
Who fills with rotten Grain his furrow'd Fields?
But culls the best that bounteous *Ceres* yields.
Thus gay the ripen'd Ears and full appear,
And a rich Harvest crowns the Tillers Care.
Art thou, Oh Man, less careful of thy Kind,
Nor what thou sow'st, nor what thou reap'st, dost
 mind?
Do's not the Beauty of thy Off-spring move
Thy Passion, with a Parent's Pride and Love?
If sound and comely thou would'st have thy Breed,
Let a sound Womb receive thy healthy Seed.
The Thund'rer's Image dost thou not respect,
Nor Nature's Laws thy cruel Heart affect?
Thou then would'st learn, what all who Love shou'd
 know,
The Field, the Seed to fit before you Sow.
Ye Pow'rs who o'er the Genial Bed preside,
Fond Wives and Husbands in their Pleasures
 guide;

CALLIPÆDIÆ.

Nor rashly let 'em try the Sweet Embrace,
Nor with corrupted Joys their House disgrace.
A Curse attends the Crime. Oh Sov'reign *Jove*,
Parent of Gods and Men, Mankind reprove;
Nor longer let their hateful Loves endure,
Chast be their Wishes, their Embraces pure,
Let a new Genius from high Heav'n descend
To Beauty and to Love alike a Friend;
For Husbands let him sacred Lessons write,
And with Success to future Times transmit.

This do's not to inform the Age suffice,
A Healthy *Hymen* is not always wise.
As well as sound, the Lover shou'd be strong,
And never to the Wrinkled wed the Young.
A Youth ne'er couple to a Wife decay'd,
Nor to a Cripple match a blooming Maid.
For ne'er the Genial Pleasure will they tast,
In vain the Youth's carest, the Maid embrac'd.
The Furies follow such unequal Vows,
And fill with endless Plagues the jarring House.
See that ill-mated Nymph, whose barter'd Charms
Are blasted in a Miser's frozen Arms.
How daily from his hated Kiss she flies,
And how her Bosom swells with secret Sighs.
From his loath'd Bed, when Day appears, she leaps,
And lonely o'er her joyless Spousals weeps.

CALLIPÆDIÆ.

Happy, Oh *Cybelle*, the *Phrygian* Boy,
Thou lov'dst, and yet excus'dst a Lovers Joy.
From an old Goddess, when her Kiss is dry,
The Youth she covets, if he's wise, will fly.
Where Beauty's wanting, Youth has often Charms,
Where-ever Youth is wanting, nothing warms;
For Juiceless Age do's youthful Sap destroy,
And wears and wastes the Strength it can't enjoy.
As oft, in *Lybian* Fields, the thirsty Sands
Suck up the Rains, and yet the burning Lands
Gape still, insatiate for the falling Show'r,
Wou'd drain the Liquid Skies, and still have more:
Thus are the Young exhausted by the old,
As Summer's Heat is chill'd by Winter's Cold.
Their Seed resists the Generative Pow'r,
And Nature do's the forc'd Embrace abhor.
For if a Child from such a Mixture's born,
His Parents Grief 'twill be, his Country's Scorn.
His languid Limbs will scarce their weight sustain,
And if it lives to Age, 'twill live in Pain.
 But all our Precepts of Success will fail,
While Int'rest, and the Lust of Gold, prevail.
Mony will still the Marriage Vow direct;
The Portion, and the Jointure, none neglect.
Our Rules to Truth may be ally'd, but who
Will change the Profitable for the True?

CALLIPÆDIÆ.

He who with dirty Acres fills a Deed,
Love where he will, shall in his Love succeed.
By Parents for their Daughter he's carest;
For him the Bowl is fill'd, the Nymph is drest.
Let him be ne'er so Ugly, or so Old,
A crowd of proffer'd Beauties tempt his Gold.
Tho' Scurffs defile his Skin, and Spots his Face,
He's welcome to the spotless Maid's Embrace.
Nor do's she, when she sees his Riches, dread
A spotted Issue from his loathsom Bed.
Tho' Crippled are his Limbs, his Head reclin'd,
And Age forbids him to encrease his Kind;
By Choice, or else Compell'd, she yields her Charms
To the cold Circle of his wither'd Arms;
Where a Wife's Privilege she ne'er shall know:
From whence what floods of Tears, what Sighs will flow?
What Nights of Wishing, and what Days of Woe.
And when her Beauty's in its brightest Bloom,
The Fires of Youth with vain Desire consume.
Or if with Fruit obscene her Bed's defil'd,
She'll mourn o'er a deform'd or sickly Child.
With Terror thus she *Hymen's* Laws obeys,
And suffers by Constraint the Loath'd Embrace;
Still dreading to behold a frightful Boy,
She dies with Fear, when she shou'd die with Joy.

CALLIPÆDIÆ.

But if a lawless Wish her Breast enflames,
No Plea's so plausible for faithless Dames.
Will she not use her Beauty in her Prime?
If old her Spouse, or ugly, where's the Crime?
She'll meet some happy Youth with fierce Delight,
And fill thy Mansion with a comely Sight.
Around thy Board the jolly Boys shall croud,
And thou, of Riches not thy own, be proud.
Here the Knight's noble Front adorns the Room,
And there's the slavish Picture of a Groom;
This Boy thy Neighbour's dull Resemblance bears,
And that the Colonel's gen'rous Image wears.
Thy Hoards descend to these, and theirs shall be
The Lands, which from thy Fathers fell to Thee.
These thy rich Pastures shall enjoy, and these,
A Foreign Race, thy Ancient Seat possess.

Nor is it thus with private Wives alone,
This Houshold Curse has often reach'd the Crown.
For when the Monarch's Manly Vigour dies,
And in his Bones some old Distemper lies,
How can he then a Royal Maid caress,
And his high Bed with legal Off-spring bless?
Thus oft a spurious Heir invades the Throne,
Or the Rule falls to a Dissembled Son.

Say, where's there such an old decrepid Witch,
So foul, and so deform'd, but if she's Rich,

CALLIPÆDIÆ.

Tho' Toothless, and Blear-ey'd, tho' Deaf and Blind,
A Youth to Woo her, and to Wed, she'll find?
If madly she the Marriage Joy desires,
And burns with impotent, but furious Fires;
He Seizes on her Wealth, and then he'll rove,
Abhor her Person, and despise her Love.
He'll bribe his Way to some young Virgin's Arms,
Or purchase a young Wife's forbidden Charms;
Riot in Joy, and revel on her Sweets,
While the Hag's groaning in her Widow'd Sheets.
Hence Quarrels, Jealousie, and Strife are bred,
And the rude Railings of a slighted Bed.
Hence Vipers she provides to fire his Blood,
And spurs his Vigour with salacious Food.
I, for these Reasons, shou'd advise to range,
But that Religion's Laws forbid to change.
Free shou'd the Pleasure be, as free the Choice,
And only Love direct the Lover's Joys:
This Nature bids. In all unequal Pairs,
However join'd, th' Election was not hers.
The sick and sound, to mingle, she dislikes,
Nor shou'd the Living with the Dying mix.
But equal be their Age, their Strength the same,
And mutual Fires their youthful Breasts enflame.
The Spring of Life let either Sex improve,
And a rich Harvest shall reward their Love.

CALLIPÆDIÆ.

Nor with green Girls shou'd beardless Boys be join'd,
The Body comes not forward like the Mind.
No Juice as yet the Genial Vessels swells,
But scatter'd in the growing Man it dwells.
Themis enjoin'd this sacred Law of old,
And still its Reason and its Virtue hold.
Twelve Springs compleat, before she thinks to wed,
Their Vernal Bloom must on the Virgin Shed;
If a ripe Child she'd to her Husband bear,
And bless him with a strong and lusty Heir.
For then, if she conceives the Genial Fruit,
The Soil has Strength to feed the spreading Root.
Her vital Heat encreases, and her Blood
Then swells within her Womb, a Rosie Flood,
From whence the future Birth imbibes its Food.
And now her swelling Breasts create Desire,
And Hills of Snow lascivious Flames inspire.
Thus when below the Viril Down begins
To mark the Males, above to shade their Chins,
Their Limbs are lusty, fit for *Hymen's* Vow,
And then they to his secret Shrine may bow.
Since Nature do's such equal Laws provide
For Marriage, let her Laws all Lovers guide;
And such shall find, who thus for Love prepare,
Their Pleasure Perfect, and their Issue Fair.

CALLIPÆDIÆ.

And now, while we our grateful Precepts spread,
While our kind Arts direct the Nuptial Bed,
Behold a lovely Youth to Manhood grown,
And on his Royal Brow the *Celtick* Crown.
The Sceptre his Magestick Fathers bore
He wields, and wears th' Imperial Robes they wore.
Lewis from high *Olympus* sent, design'd
To Rule with Righteous sway, and bless Mankind.
What shining Graces in his Bloom are seen,
What Sov'reign Beauty, what a Godlike Mien?
His lofty Look reveals his mighty Mind,
And all that's Great with all that's Fair is join'd.
A thousand Goddesses, with wishing Eyes,
Survey him, and for him the Fairest sighs.
For him the beauteous Nymph of *Austria's* Line,
Her Form Celestial, as her Race divine,
For whom the *Taijo* flows a Golden Stream,
In her Chast Bosom feels a kindling Flame.
With rival Wishes, and as warm Desires,
The Royal *Lusitanian* Maid expires.
For him *Hesperian* Nymphs and *Teuton* sigh,
For him a thousand Heav'nly Virgins die.
But thou, Oh Hope of *Gaul*, do'st wisely weigh
Th' Important Int'rests of thy Regal Sway;
Nor wilt thou chuse, too eager of the Bliss,
That for her Race, or for her Beauty this;

CALLIPÆDIÆ.

The Virtues of the Mind thou most do'st prize,
And lik'st the Soul before thou lik'st the Eyes.
What a mad Custom now with Monarchs spreads?
For Brides unseen are brought to Genial Beds.
With others Eyes Imperial Maids are view'd,
And easily with others Lips are woo'd.
But let us pray, that Heav'n wou'd crown thy Vows
With the fair Issue of a charming Spouse.
What gains the Peoples Hearts, what moves them more,
Than matchless Beauty join'd with matchless Pow'r?
When a bright Crown a lovely Brow adorns,
Their fond Obedience then to Worship turns.
When Beauty brightens the Majestick Mien,
The King's a God, a Goddess then the Queen.
What if a Virgin boasts a Princely Race,
Or a proud *Juno* fills a King's Embrace?
If foul her Person, and deform'd her Face,
What Love can she create, but what will stain
The Throne with Heirs, and curse the coming Reign?
How apt are Kings, in their Amours, to Rove?
How soon they loath a faithful Consort's Love?
The Royal Wanton scorns his sacred Vows,
And with a spurious Race defiles his House.
Thus *Jove*, with *Juno's* cold Embraces cloy'd,
Deflow'r'd the Nymphs, the willing Wives enjoy'd.

CALLIPÆDIÆ.

With a base Off-spring he disgrac'd the Skies;
And Kings, like him, permitted Joys despise.
Do thou this Guilt and this Dishonour shun,
And love a loving Wife, and her alone.
Thy House with beauteous Issue thus encrease,
And with a God-like Heir thy Empire bless.
   Were I to meddle with such sacred Things,
And by my Thoughts presume to guide a King's,
Thou a fair Virgin of a Race Divine
Shou'dst chuse, a Nymph, whose Ways agree with
       thine,
To sooth thy Royal Cares; not one whose Sire
Wou'd bribe thy Friendship with a fatal Fire.
Who to a falling Throne wou'd be ally'd,
And purchase, with his Kingdom's Peace, a Bride?
A Consort seek in some Imperial Court,
Whose Monarch needs no Neighbour's vain Support;
Who by his proper Might his Pow'r maintains,
And with an Independant Empire Reigns.
While *Cæsar* meditates the Marriage Joys,
And friendly Fates direct his happy Choice,
My Labour, *Phœbus* fav'ring, I'll pursue,
And for the Wedded Pairs my Toil renew.

CALLIPÆDIÆ.

BOOK II.

THE Rites perform'd, the Nymph's no longer coy,
But, like the Bridegroom, burns to taste the Joy.
The chearful Parents load the Festial Board,
And empty, for the Bride, the Golden Hoard.
The Father most, with a dilated Soul,
Deals freely to the Guests the flowing Bowl.
The Table's with inverted Glasses spread,
And the gay Lass the measur'd Round is led.
The venal Harper tears his labour'd Strings,
While the glad House with Bridal Blessings rings.
The Bridegroom steals a Pledge of future Bliss,
And oft he mixes with his Mirth a Kiss.

CALLIPÆDIÆ.

Such lawful Love the Marriage God will Crown,
Such Joys, the Moons Compleat, will *Juno* own.
Minerva's Manners, and *Diana's* Vows,
Are now a Jest to his impatient Spouse.
Thou, *Venus*, art her only Goddess, now
To thee she'll only kneel, and pay her Vow.
The Queen of Beauty thou, the Queen of Love,
Ador'd by men, and ev'n confest by *Jove*.
To thee we owe our sweetest, best Delights;
To thee our joyous Days, and blissful Nights.
To thee the *Phrygian* Shepherd gave the Prize,
And proudly didst thou bear his Judgment to the Skies,
His Praise, his Pref'rence, in the fam'd Dispute,
To thee was sweeter than the Golden Fruit.
Fierce *Juno's* Rage, and chast *Minerva's*, he
Despis'd, and only fix'd his Eyes on thee.
Thee *Phœbus* has confess'd, thee Sov'reign *Jove*,
Thee all the Pow'rs below, and all above.
No Bounds did they prescribe to their Desires,
But oft with Steril burn'd, and Impious Fires.
Th' *Oebalian* Boy the God of Light enjoy'd,
And him unwitting in his Play destroy'd.
By Thee the King of Gods enflam'd, possest
The Nymphs, the Youth, and whom he pleas'd carest.

CALLIPÆDIÆ.

The sullen Doatard now forgets his Years,
And laughs, and now the rev'rend Matron lears.
But evening Shades to Lovers Joys invite,
When *Venus* rises with her beamy Light.
Hence Modesty awhile, let Love succeed,
And chastly revel in the Genial Bed.
Ye Mothers, who the pleasing Fights have known,
Attend the Fair, and loose her Virgin Zone.
Now to the Bride the naked Bridegroom turns,
And, to begin the Marriage Combat, burns.
Come to my Arms, my Love, my Life, he cries,
While trembling by his Side the Damsel lies.
Th' unwelcome Croud are gone, the Field is ours,
Oh, waste not with delay these precious Hours.
Come to my arms, and *Hymen's* happy Fight,
And give to Love and me the blissful Night.
But stay, too furious Youth, nor yet engage,
Awhile command thy Heat, and check thy Rage.
If Meats thy Belly fill, or Fumes thy Head,
Defer the Raptures of the Nuptial Bed.
When indigested Meals thy Stomach Load,
Delay thy Off'ring to the Marriage God,
For thin will be the Seed; the Work will prove,
As crude and unconcocted as thy Love.
Stay 'till the gen'rous Juice has reach'd thy Veins,
And a clean Stomach fills thy flowing Reins.

CALLIPÆDIÆ.

This Lesson will to Lovers seem severe,
But practis'd well, their Issue shall be fair.
  Nature, who to improve her Kind is wise,
Prefers the fresh Embrace, and Morning Joys.
The *Fœtus* thus a fairer Form receives,
And in the Child the Genial Beauty lives.
The Reason this. For when the Humid Night,
With her black Mantle, veils the Golden Light,
When on the weary Limbs sweet Sleep descends,
Restores the Man, and Life and Love befriends,
Then Inward sinks the Heat, digested Food
Supplies the lab'ring Veins with vig'rous Blood;
And these the generative Vessels load
With Juices, to regale the Nuptial God.
A finer Spirit's to the Seed convey'd,
And a new Store to Nature's Treasure laid.
New Heat, new Strength, the Crimson Flood supplies,
And fresh as opening Day the lusty Bridegrooms rise.
Remember then a rash Embrace to shun,
Nor madly to the secret Rapture run,
Lest Nature's Work by too much haste be spoil'd,
And thy blind Lust shou'd wrong the coming Child:
As *Jove* his own Immortal Race defil'd,
When with crude Nectar he his Wife carest,
And with Precipitated Transports blest:

CALLIPÆDIÆ.

From whence foul *Vulcan* to his Horror sprung,
And the rude God from Heav'ns high Arch he flung.
His Limbs distorted, and deform'd his Face,
Refus'd at the Immortal Board a Place,
The Jest of Heav'n, and by his Sire deny'd
The Bed of *Pallas*, whom he wish'd his Bride,
Love's Mother on the Cripple was bestow'd;
The fairest Goddess on the foulest God.
Despis'd and hated, he possest her Charms,
And dirted with his Filth her loathing Arms.
Thus oft, by cruel Fathers hard Commands,
The fairest to the foulest give their Hands.
From whence the Marriage lawful Joy's refus'd,
And the chaste Bed with lawless Bliss abus'd.

Nor is't enough, that, while your Meals digest,
You leave the willing Beauty uncarest;
Nor that you don't, by too much haste, destroy
The genuine Warmth, which makes a fruitful Joy.
This you as well shou'd know. Observe with care
The Face of Heav'n, when you embrace the Fair.
It more avails than when the Boy is born,
The Moon's Increase to mark, or wayning Horn.
What Sign has the Ascendant, how the Skies
Look, when the Babe begins his Infant Cries.
Mark rather what Celestial Aspect shines,
When the good Seed to form the *Fœtus* joins:

CALLIPÆDIÆ.

What friendly Stars their happy Influence shed
On the young Birth, aud rule the Genial Bed.
But who shou'd hope to be for Fate too wise,
Or search into the Secrets of the Skies,
Or Heav'n or Earth disclose to mortal Eyes?
Thou, bright *Urania*, thou alone canst tell,
How roll the Spheres, and how they Work reveal,
Nor Earth from thee, nor Heav'n, the Gods conceal.
Inspire the lab'ring Muse, for fair's the Field,
And a rich Crop of deathless Fame 'twill yield.
If thou'lt direct her how to view the Sky,
And the Stars Motions to our World apply.

For who that does with wondring Eyes behold
Yon Arch of Heav'n, when gilt with streams of Gold,
Yon sparkling Orbs, whose num'rous Fires confound
Our Eyes, still rolling with a rapid Round,
Can think th' Omnipotent has spread in vain
Those Radiant Wonders, on th' Etherial Plain?
Eternal Wisdom something more design'd,
Than a gay Picture to divert Mankind.
Dost thou not see, when sev'ral Stars arise,
How Earth's affected by the vary'd Skies?
How Wind, how Rain, how Heat or Cold prevail,
And Ships on Smiling Seas, or stormy, sail?
That with the *Hyades* wet Tempests rise,
And windy with *Orion*, who denies?

CALLIPÆDIÆ.

Or that the thirsty *Dog* leaves bare the Sands,
Sucks up the Springs, and burns the barren Lands?
What need I Heav'ns Imperial Spheres survey,
That rule o'er Mortals with resistless Sway;
Or bloody *Jove's*, or *Saturn's* fatal Star,
Or fiery *Mars*, that breathes eternal War?
If *Leo* joins his raging Fires with theirs,
What Ruin it creates, what Impious Wars?
What Crouds it to the Cruel Fates decrees,
What Changes in the smiling Face of Peace?
Free States to Tyrants by their Influence yield,
And lawless Monarchs ravish'd Sceptres wield.
From such Conjunctions *Rome's* Misfortunes rose;
Pompey and *Cæsar* thus, of old, were Foes.
Thessalian Fields with *Roman* Blood were stain'd,
And *Rome* that Empire lost which *Cæsar* gain'd.
Ev'n now from Heav'n such baleful Influence falls,
Which drives th' *Iberians* on the Martial *Gauls;*
To mutual Wounds their adverse Kings excites,
And each, because the Stars compel him, Fights.
For *Mars* his Fires with *Jove's* and *Saturn's* blends,
Where the fierce *Centaur* his red Arms extends.
And as malignant Stars to bloody Fights
Provoke, so they corrupt Love's soft Delights
With Plagues, the World with foul Contagion fill,
And here the Race defile, as there they kill.

CALLIPÆDIÆ.

Sickness, if *Mars* in *Cancer*, dread, and Foes,
Or if his livid Hue old *Saturn* shews.
Why shou'd I search into such sacred things,
The course of Fate disclose, and secret Springs?
Enough for me, what makes a lovely Heir,
As far as *Phœbus* teaches to declare.

'Tis Fam'd that Men in ancient Times were griev'd,
And beg'd of Heav'n, and cry'd to be reliev'd.
Ill-shapen Births in ev'ry Clime appear'd,
And the whole Race a full Corruption fear'd.
Or what unfriendly Skies, or noxious Seed,
Produc'd this Ill to Man, and stain'd the Breed,
Who knows? but, if we credit Fame, 'twas rare
A Man to meet, or Woman, that was Fair.
  When from high Heav'n the Thund'rer *Jove*
    survey'd
Mankind, and saw their Beauty thus decay'd,
A Council to attend him he Commands,
Of all who favour'd *Hymen's* holy Bands.
Streight to his Palace, in the Inmost Sky,
The Gods and Goddesses obedient fly,
First *Juno*, by her painted Peacocks known,
Appears, and takes her Seat aside the Throne.
To Council next fair *Cytherea* moves
In her gay Chariot, drawn by Harnest Doves.

CALLIPÆDIÆ.

Her *Ceres* follows with her fruitful Train,
Queen of the Harvest and the Golden Grain.
Oh Goddess, who can Love without thy aid,
Or with a strong Embrace oblige the willing Maid!
Apollo's Presence the great Council crown'd.
Heav'n thus Assembled, and the King enthron'd,
The Gods and Goddesses around him sat,
And briefly he declar'd for what they met.
Man's wretched State he shew'd, and how his Race
Grew foul, and was his own and Heav'ns Disgrace.
When *Jove* the Matter thus had open laid,
The Gods attentive, he requir'd their Aid,
And bad them speak; and thus *Apollo* said.
Man has, ye Deities, contemn'd the Skies,
And scorn'd the Stars that teach him to be wise:
The rolling Spheres revenge his Impious Scorn,
Hence horrid Boys and hateful Girls are born.
As from my Heav'n the shining Orbs impend,
This Planet is a Foe, and that a Friend.
'Tis mine, or Strength, or Beauty to bestow,
Which few have known, or fewer wish to know;
Where Heav'n is by the Oblique Zodiack bound,
Twelve starry Signs perform their destin'd Round.
Hence ev'ry Beauty rises, ev'ry Grace,
Hence ev'ry Vice and Blemish of the Face.

CALLIPÆDIÆ.

For if to Sow the Nuptial Tiller tries,
When Horny *Helles* first ascends the Skies,
Whatever Wife shall then Conceive, she'll bear
A Child that shall disgrace the Nurse's Care;
Short-neck'd, and Bandy-legg'd, will be the Birth,
And rarely will he raise his Eyes from Earth.
His Snowy Locks shall hide his Beetle Skull,
And the vile Lump be both deform'd and dull.
But most, if *Saturn's* cruel Star shall chance
On the curst Boy his gloomy Beams to glance,
If *Mars* behold him with a blasting Eye,
All Beauty then from ev'ry Part shall fly,
And ne'er in *Aries* let him rule the Sky.

 Nor *Taurus* more with Loves Delights agrees,
And most his Radiant Horns forbid increase,
In Opposition to the *Pleiades*.
Tho' fair the Daughters of fair *Pleione*,
As beauteous they, tho' ne'er so beauteous she,
Not kinder are they to a charming Face;
But when our *Cynthia* lends her gentle Rays,
And smooths the Skin, and gives the Limbs a
  grace.
To *Taurus* we return; deform'd and dull
Is he, whose Birth's beneath th' Ascendent Bull.
Long will his Nose and wide his Nostrils be,
With Goggle and with Gorgon Eyes he'll see;

CALLIPÆDIÆ.

His Fore-head ugly, thick his greasie Neck,
Yellow will be his Hair, his Eye-lids Black.
His Voice be Hoarse, and all his filthy Frame
Be, to his Parents, and his Kind, a shame.

But when the *Twins* the friendly Skies ascend,
These, ev'ry Good, and ev'ry Grace attend.
One was on Earth the *Spartan* Brothers Mind,
Beauteous themselves, they're still to Beauty kind,
So *Jove* decreed when he their Place assign'd
Amid the Stars; and gave to Rule above,
To the fair Fruit of *Leda's* injur'd Love:
The Product of the Marriage Joy they bless
With ev'ry Charm, which either Sex possess.
Not smiling Looks alone, and sparkling Eyes,
And what in Shape, or in Complexion, lies.
But their kind Influence to the Mind imparts,
Mild Manners, pleasant Wit, and pleasing Arts.
When with the *Twins* the Son of *Maia* rules,
O'er Letters they preside, and guide the Schools.
The Seeds of Eloquence they sow, and teach
A graceful Language, and a moving Speech;
The Mind and Body are at once compleat,
Soft ev'ry Word, and ev'ry Gesture sweet.

But how unlike are horrid *Cancer's* Rays,
They soil the Seed, and curse the promis'd Race.

CALLIPÆDIÆ.

Baleful with him the foul *Aselli* rise,
And the fierce *Chelæ* vex the guilty Skies:
Hence Limbs deform'd are seen, and little Eyes,
Hump-backs, huge Paunches, and uneven Teeth,
A filthy Range, and hence a Stinking-breath,
Lank dangling Arms, a short and crooked Shape,
A Shame to Nature, and the Nurse's Lap.
He who once rag'd in the *Nemæan* Wood,
The leading Labour of the lab'ring God,
Whom only *Hercules*'s Club cou'd tame,
Now burns the Skies with a malignant Flame.
And hence, when *Leo's* Lord, are Sandy Locks,
Broad Breasts, long Shanks, and stern and haughty
    Looks.
What can a Beast, or Good, or Fair, bestow,
As fell above, as he was fierce below.
His Savage Nature he in Heav'n retains,
As when on Earth he scowr'd the *Argive* Plains.
Had Fate to me, when Nature sow'd her Seed,
Beneath this Sky, a Royal Crown decreed,
The Lion's Fierceness I had still retain'd,
Rag'd in the Throne, and like a Savage reign'd.
  Astræa follows with a train of Light,
A Virgin fair as Youth, as Beauty bright,
On Earth she govern'd in the Golden Age,
E'er Pow'r prevail'd, and Wrong began to rage.

CALLIPÆDIÆ.

Where *Virgo* glitters with her sparkling Beams,
There Light, to rival *Jove's*, from *Spica* streams.
No purer Fires in all the *Zodiack* shine,
And freely now the Marry'd Pairs may join.
Their Influence on the Seed their Brightness leaves,
And the rich Womb a beauteous Birth receives.
Firm Limbs from hence, and graceful Shapes shall rise,
And Rose and Lilly Looks, and Charming Eyes.

Nor less, where *Libra* holds her equal Scale,
The finer Parts of Human Seed prevail.
Here thou, the Queen of Graces, fix'dst thy House,
To bless with friendly Beams the Teeming Spouse.
Fair Maids, and lovely Boys, from hence we see,
Who owe their Beauty and their Strength to thee.
If *Saturn* in this House shou'd chance to shine,
And with his dusky Light defile the Sign,
The same dull Colour on the Seed he sheds,
And where he Rules, his Leaden Mantle spreads.
But *Cytherea* adds to *Lybra's* Charms,
And forms a Heav'nly Fair for *Hymen's* Arms.

Who, when the *Scorpion*, with his spiral Pride,
Does o'er the Signs in the Ascendant ride,
Wou'd fill with fatal Seed th' Incautious Bride?
When with his Pois'nous Tail he sweeps the Skies,
He darts his Venom on the Bridal Joys.

CALLIPÆDIÆ.

From hence, Splay-feet and Bandy-leggs proceed,
A Ferret Eye from hence, a Yellow Head.
The Monster, whose vile Beams infect the
    Blood,
Who owes his Being to the stagnant Flood,
Retains the Nature of his Parent Mud.
  Not *Chiron* thus, *Achilles* Master, sways
The subject World, with his ascendant Rays.
Him Piety in Heav'n a Place assign'd,
And there with pious Care he rules Mankind.
For when he rises, if you sow the Seed,
A Nervous Arm he forms, a beauteous Head,
And hence the Limbs are strong, the Shoulders
    spread.
But if his starry Tail the *Centaur* shows,
The Birth will ill Reward the Mother's Throws,
  When the dull *Goat* do's in the *Zodiack* browse,
And heavy *Saturn's* in his Sleepy House,
The Fruit which such ill-omen'd Seed shall bear,
Will scarce, when born, in any Part be fair.
  And now the *Phrygian* Youth his Urn extends,
The Seed he blesses; and the Fruit befriends.
  Aquarius wayning, *Pisces* mount their Sign,
And in one House their watry Influence join.
Hence Weakness, little Heads, a dwarfish Size,
Lean Limbs, and a distorted Figure rise.

CALLIPÆDIÆ.

What shall we of the wandring Planets say,
And how the sublunary World they sway?
Who knows not, when they Thwart, and when they Join,
They Work? How kind a *Sextile*, or a *Trine*.
If *Jove* in a propitious House appears,
And *Venus* mixes Rays with friendly Stars;
The King of Heav'n, the *Cyprian* Queen, will spread
The Loves and Graces on the Genial Bed.
 Nor are we ign'rant, that a Vernal Joy
Conduces to a fair and lusty Boy.
When Nature paints the Meads, and cloaths the Trees,
And all her living Works at once increase,
Strongly the generative Juices rise,
The whole Creation feels the warmer Skies,
And smiles, and shoots aloft, as Winter dies.
But when the Summer Heat severely burns,
The Chyle's corrupted, and to Choller turns,
The Spirits flag, the vital Strength decays,
And faintly will you run the Nuptial Race.
No kindly Heat from *Autumn* Suns descend,
And less do frigid Winds the Seed befriend.
 Oh Mortals, curb your Wishes, and be wise,
Enjoy the happy Night in happy Skies.

CALLIPÆDIÆ.

And then to *Hymen* if you Homage pay,
For a fair Off-spring you Foundations lay.
 The Gods agreed; and now, by *Jove's* Command,
These Precepts in Etherial Records stand.
What *Phœbus* said, the Heav'nly Councils Sign,
And stampt it with the Seal of Laws Divine.
To me *Urania* their high Acts imparts,
As pleasant Hers, as the most pleasing Arts.
 You then, Ambitious of a Father's Name,
Who feed a regular, and pious Flame,
Who the next Age in Beauty wou'd improve,
And have your Issue both your Pride and Love,
Attend, and learn the proper time to sow
The Seed, that fair the future Fruit may grow,
Observe th' ascending and declining Stars,
In what Conjunction, *Saturn*, *Jove*, or *Mars*;
And how the Sun's with *Venus*, or the Moon:
An easie Art, and may be master'd soon.
But if on this you'd not employ your Mind,
In Tables rightly drawn, the Hour you'll find;
Where daily you may mark, in ev'ry Clime,
The Sign that Courts to Love, and hit the Time.
 Nor is't enough a happy Sky to know,
To mark the Sign, and hit the time to Sow;
In *Hymen's* Rites are other things to learn,
Ye marry'd Pairs! and of as high Concern.

CALLIPÆDIÆ.

Howe'er Desire may to the Joy excite,
When the Months flow, forbear the dear Delight;
For the foul *Menstruæ* kill the Genial Juice,
Or Births abortive and obscene produce.
And as the foolish Tiller toils in vain,
Who sows in drunken Fields the rotting Grain;
No ripen'd Ear will e'er reward his Pain:
So he who sheds in humid Cells his Seed,
Or wastes his Vigour, or defiles his Breed.
How wretched is the Child, how stain'd with Sores?
It sucks the Latent Filth at all its Pores.
The Root corrupted, when the Fruit appears,
In ev'ry Part the venom'd Marks it wears.
For what's more Pois'nous than this Female Flood?
The dregs of Life, and skimmings of the Blood.
If it shou'd chance to touch the tender Fruit,
Fall on the Springing Vine, or Planted Sprout,
It blasts like Lightning; shou'd a greedy Cur,
As foul his Hunger as the Feast's Impure,
Swallow the Filth, he's streight with Madness seiz'd,
And with his horrid Bite infects the rest.
Despise, ye Marry'd Pairs! such Joys obscene,
And the Seed sprinkle, when the Womb is clean.
You, ye fond Wives, who love the rapt'rous Bliss,
To feel the close Embrace, and biting Kiss,

CALLIPÆDIÆ.

Too gamesome at the Sport, the Work you spoil,
Too quick rebound, and when you play, you toil.
You heave too fast, the flowing Seed prevent,
And the Male Vigour with the Force is spent.
What reaches in a refluent Tide returns,
Or the balkt Womb the swift Prevention mourns.
If in its Cell, the Seed, thus shaken, sticks,
The *Fœtus* cannot, for your Frisking, fix.
Both yield in vain, what Nature wou'd supply,
And the loose Parts in scatter'd Masses lye.
Nor will your Wishes with an Heir be bless'd,
But your strong Youth in fruitless Joys you'll waste.

 Hence, ye Profane! We write not this to you,
Who, with hot Lust, our harmless Verse will view.
You'll lewdly Nature's hidden Works survey,
Or scoff the sacred Womb where once you lay
Hence, hence, while we to chaster Eyes expose
Her teeming Pow'rs, and Genuine Form disclose.

 Beneath the void *Abdomen's* lowest Space,
Distinct, this little Cell do's Nature place.
Form'd like a Pear, and like a Purse the Skin
Is Ductile, that the Birth may stretch within.
The Artery this, the Nerve, and double Vein,
With Blood and Spirits from the Stock maintain.
From the whole Body 'tis with both supply'd,
And call'd the Womb, and goes from side to side.

CALLIPÆDIÆ.

From Right to Left it thus directly runs,
The Left for Daughters, and the Right for
    Sons.
An Oblong Pipe is at the bottom plac'd,
By which the Viril Nerve is oft embrac'd;
The Seed is darted to the Womb by this,
The Center of the Mother's Pain and Bliss.
'Tis call'd the Neck, and in the strong Embrace,
It shuts, with wond'rous Art, the Parent place,
Lest the hot Youth too far shou'd wildly rove,
And ravage the forbidden Fields of Love.
When the Male Seed has past this narrow Room,
It meets the Female in the sucking Womb.
When clinging Arms th' ejected Juice compel,
It darts and lodges in the gaping Cell.
For as, with Joy, the famish'd Paunch receives
The grateful Food which Nature's Wants relieves,
So the glad Womb repletes her empty Maw,
And both their Fill with greedy Suction draw.
Light Motions hence, and nimble Hips, destroy
The Tillers Pains, and mar a fruitful Joy.
Let's second now those Parents pious Vows,
Who pray for Sons, and hate a Female House;
And teach, to get a Boy, the teeming Spouse.
Males are the Strength and Glory of a Race,
And Female Issue curst by some, as base;

CALLIPÆDIÆ.

Nature, unwilling, gives to Woman Birth,
And with fair Monsters loads the burthen'd Earth.
An Error this; for common Sense allows,
That Sex is best to whom the other bows.
But let us, leaving this Debate, our Theam
Pursue, and tell how Wives with Males may Teem;
To fill with Manly Heirs each Royal Court,
And the high Lineage of the World support.
Those most are apt for Males, in whom there meet
Most of Male Vigour, and the Vital Heat.
This the Learn'd tell us, and Experience shews,
That Manly Thoughts to Manly Love dispose.
A bold, a gen'rous, and an easie Mind,
Assist the Sex, to propagate the Kind.
That future *Hymen's* may not strive for Boys
In vain, nor covet Heirs with fruitless Joys,
Reason directs, that in the choice of Food,
The Parents carefully prepare their Blood.
Who knows not that the Purple Veins produce
The Genial Seed, which once was Purple Juice.
But the new Spirits change their guilty Dye,
And white into the Womb, and rich they fly.
With vigorous Juices if you feed your Veins,
With Sap and Vigour they supply the Reins.
Nor Windy shou'd they be, nor free from Wind,
For a soft Vapour to the Womb is kind.

CALLIPÆDIÆ.

Nor shun the strutting Dug, nor spare the Pail,
Since a white Meal's Propitious to the Male.
Give to these Precepts, in thy Heart, a Place,
And Masculine expect thy promis'd Race.
But why to Diet you shou'd I pretend,
Since Nature's to your Sex so much a Friend?
Rich Meals for you, ye Bridegrooms, she provides,
And warming Draughts to chear your wishing Brides.
Sufficient for the Nuptial Joy's the Vine,
And lusty Boys are got by gen'rous Wine.
But most, Oh *Burgundy!* thy Nectar warms
Their Hearts, and burnishes their Bridal Arms.
Both bright *Champagne* with equal Vigour fills,
And the rich Cluster of the *Aisian* Hills.

And you, ye Wives, who with your Husbands join,
To pray for Sons to prop an Ancient Line,
At Meals, with sparkling Wine rejoice your Souls,
And freely pledge 'em in their modest Bowls.
Nature, by this, the Genial Heat will feed,
And urge the Womb to seize the Manly Seed.
By this for Males 'tis fitted; but beware,
And ben't too lavish, as you shou'd not spare.
For when the Soil's with too much Moisture drench'd,
The Native Warmth in both alike is quench'd.
Nor have they Strength, when they to *Hymen* pay
Their Vows, Foundations for strong Males to lay.

CALLIPÆDIÆ.

Avoid, when flush'd with Wine, the Marriage Bliss,
Nor soil your Pleasures by a drunken Kiss.
For filthy Births, such indigested Seed,
And future Gouts, and knotty Joints, will breed.
Let Reason in your Cups direct your Draught;
The Ship is often sunk when over Fraught.

Nor shou'd you only of full Bowls beware,
But too much Love, as well as Wine, forbear,
If you your Race wou'd honour with an Heir.
Repeated Joys corrupt the Native Heat,
And Wheyey Seed assumes the Genial Seat.
A Female Child deceives the Father's Hopes,
And the Stock withers, and the Lineage drops.

With Temper when you run the Nuptial Race,
Nor with a second, spoil the first Embrace;
Compleatly when you'r arm'd for *Hymen's* Wars,
Observe, ye Marry'd Pairs, the reigning Stars.
And if they are to Males or Females kind,
If warm or cold, and how oppos'd or join'd.
For Masculine we call the warmer Skies,
And Male will be the Product of your Joys.
When the Ram rules, or when the Lion shines,
Or when the Ballance, Centaur, or the Twins,
Or when the Radiant Urn its Light displays,
A Boy expect to crown the close Embrace.

CALLIPÆDIÆ.

The Rolling Planets are to Males inclin'd,
As in the Lessons of the Learn'd we find.
Thus *Saturn*, furious *Mars*, and Sov'reign *Jove*,
Reward with Boys the Parents faithful Love.
The same do'st thou, Oh *Phœbe*, Queen of Night,
To Mortals lavish of thy Silver Light.
As oft as *Jove* is in the Manly Signs,
Or *Titan* there with Golden Glories shines,
Who Love's Career with Vigour then shall run,
For him *Latona* brings a welcome Son.

A Morning Joy will sprightly Males produce,
For Rest and Sleep invigorate the Juice.
This in the Womb a firm Foundation lays,
Which will in time a Manly Structure raise.

Nor is't enough for Women to receive
The Grain, the Tillers for their Harvest give.
Male-Fruit as well from other Causes springs,
And other Care a Manly Issue brings.
For, when the Grain into the Ground is thrown,
And, with the Male, the Female Seed is sown,
On the Right-side the Mother shou'd recline;
For a right Womb preserves the Father's Line.
Most to the Right the living Heat subsides,
There Nature, best to feed the Birth, provides.
The Left is weak, and thence, as say the Wise,
On the Right-side the Male Conception lyes.

CALLIPÆDIÆ.

From a Left Womb a Female Issue flows,
And from a Right a Male, as there it grows.
By Art, when Nature may be here supply'd,
The weaker Testicle is firmly ty'd.
That a right Flood may fill the fertile Womb;
Nor from the Left the Genial Deluge come.
Thus when the Farmer for the teeming Year
Wou'd Yoke, in time, an Ox, or strain a Steer;
He ties the Bull before he leaps the Cow,
That a Male Calf may vex the painful Plow.
For a Male Issue is the gen'ral Care,
A Boy the Mother's Hope, the Father's Pray'r.
What shall we here of wicked Postures say?
When Lovers with Inverted Dalliance play;
Nor take the Joy, as Nature bids the Bliss,
But to the Pillow turn the Balmy Kiss.
What Monsters spring from such impure Delights?
What hideous Forms? What foul Hermaphrodites?
But the chast Muse forbids me to declare
What the chast Wife wou'd blush to do, or hear.
Stop, stop thy wanton Pen, she cries, and shew,
With Modest Art, what Modest Wives may do.
The Muses no Lascivious Words allow,
Nor he, who ne'er to *Hymen* paid his Vow.
Nor must I on his secret Rites prolong
My Theam; for now the *Fœtus* claims my Song.

CALLIPÆDIÆ.

BOOK III.

 LATE Conception, when by Signs you know,
As chiefly when the Months forbear to flow,
When the kind Wife with fiercer Rapture dies,
And faster in the Transport shuts her Eyes;
When the Womb closes, and the rising Flood
Extend the swelling Breasts with vary'd Blood;
Betimes the careful Mother shou'd prepare
To breed the future Birth, and bring it fair.
For oft, by Negligence, the Teeming Wife
Cripples the Child, and curses it with Life.

Since Nature's Depths, with Pleasure, we explore,
Whate'er we know, are fond of knowing more;

CALLIPÆDIÆ.

Since we no Art can to Perfection bring,
Nor teach, but when we trace it from the Spring:
How in the Womb the fair Conception grows,
And how it there increases, we'll disclose.

   Ye sacred Nymphs, who haunt th' *Aonian* Grove,
Forgive the Muse, that speaks so oft of Love.
Again, she's forc'd the Marriage Bliss to name,
To shock your Ears, as she provokes your Shame.
Yet wanton Images she wou'd not raise,
And Sings, but as the Theam compels her Layes.
Love is to Love the greatest Plague; it spoils
The Work, and with new Joys the Past defiles.
The Seed conceiv'd is by new Seed destroy'd,
She'll teem too much, who is too much enjoy'd.
Thus a new Burthen hurts the growing Child,
And a new *Fœtus* on the old is pil'd;
Or, scarce Conceiv'd, Abortions oft chastize,
The frisking Motions, and repeated Joys.
As when in Spring the ruddy Cherry blooms,
And fragrant Flow'rs the fruitful Grove perfumes,
If a rude hand shou'd shake the tender Boughs,
In vain the Year his Vernal Beauty blows;
No Summer Fruit fulfils the Virgin's Hopes,
To Earth the Promis'd Feast Unripen'd drops.
So none repeats too oft the dear Embrace,
But for the Pleasure she severely pays.

CALLIPÆDIÆ.

Not the she Wolf, nor filthy Female Goat,
With Teeming Bellies, with their Males will Rut.
  To feed, I now shou'd teach the Pregnant Fair,
And tell what Food to chuse, and what forbear.
What Diet's to the *Fœtus* kind, and what
Is noxious. This they ev'ry where are taught.
The Rules are neither rare, nor Precepts few,
And I my chiefest Point must now pursue.
  When in the Womb the Forming Infant Grows,
And swelling Beauties shew a Teeming Spouse;
All Melancholly, Spleen, and anxious Care,
All Sights Obscene, that shock the Eyes, forbear.
But a fair Picture, and a beauteous Face,
By Fancy's mighty Pow'r, refine the Race.
The Spirits to the Brain the Form convey,
Which thence the Seed receives, while Nature works her way.
On ev'ry Part th' Imprinted Image stays,
And with the *Fœtus* grows the borrow'd Grace.
Strong are the Characters which Fancy makes,
And good, and bad, the ripe Conception takes.
As when the Wheaten Mass is work'd to Dough,
Or swells with Leaven in the Kneading-Trough,
It takes whatever Marks the Maker gives,
And from the Baker's Hand its Form receives.

CALLIPÆDIÆ.

So works the Fancy on the Female Mold,
And Women shou'd beware what they behold.
Nor New is the Remark, of Old we find,
That Births were thus affected by the Mind.
As from without an Object, fair or foul,
With Terror, or with Pleasure, struck the Soul.
  Who, *Chiron*, has not of thy Monstrous Birth
Been told? and how thy Form disgrac'd the
    Earth?
Fair *Phyllyra*, for her Misfortunes fam'd,
Old *Saturn*'s Breast with furious Love enflam'd.
Fierce was his Fire, nor cou'd he long sustain
The burning Fever, nor resist the Pain:
But Snares he to surprize the Damsel laid,
And, as the Gods were wont, deflow'r'd the Maid.
On the Sea-shore, for Ocean was her Sire,
He chanc'd to find her with a Virgin Quire;
And as she frolick'd near the foamy Flood,
He seiz'd the Nymph, and bore her to a Wood,
A Devious Path——But Oh! what Storms of Sighs
Broke from her Breast? what Fountains from her
    Eyes?
As in the Letcher's horrid Arms she lay,
And found her Honour to his Lust a Prey.
So piercing were her Groans, her moving Cries,
They rent the Air, and reach'd the distant Skies.

CALLIPÆDIÆ.

Her; Mother *Cybele* both heard and saw,
And her lewd Husband breaking *Hymen*'s Law:
Soon from *Olympus* to the Shade she flies,
And rushes on him in his Impious Joys.
When *Saturn* fear'd she wou'd surprise the Rape;
He streight assum'd a Horse's fouler Shape,
The Fury of his Jealous Wife to 'scape.
His Lust fulfill'd, he hid him in the Shade,
And left to her Despair the Ravish'd Maid.
But ah! The Beauty of the Virgin Flow'r
Is vanish'd, and its Spring returns no more:
Nor has he with a lovely Off-spring blest
Her lab'ring Womb, nor like a God carest.
When the Nine Moons their wonted Course have run,
A Monster comes, when she expects a Son.
Oh Horror! All his lower Parts appear
A Horse, and see his Hoofs, his Tail and Hair.
But who can tell the tender Mother's Moans?
To wail her own Dishonour, and her Son's.
Ye *Nereids!* say how ev'ry sounding Shore
Your Sister's Shame did, in her Son's, deplore.
What Tides of Tears disturb'd your smiling Waves,
While thus against the Lustful God she raves.

Was't not enough my Purity to soil,
But must thou with a Beast my Womb defile,

CALLIPÆDIÆ.

A Birth Obscene? Ah! why did I survive
Thy filthy Rape? and why to bear it, Live?
Ah! why, *Latona*, didst thou aid my Throws,
And ease my Burthen, to encrease my Woes?
What Plagues for me has angry Heav'n in Store?
Had I not known enough, ye Pow'rs before,
But ah! what am I still to suffer more?
She said; and, with excess of Sorrow spent,
Her Trouble grows at last too big for vent.
Faint is her Voice, and Languid are her Eyes;
She sinks, she falls, and in appearance dies:
The mournful Sisters with Officious Care
Attend, and sudden Remedies prepare.
Rich Cordials through her Teeth by force they pour,
And with diluted Amber Life restore.
Old *Ocean* from his secret Stores supplies
The Balm, which on his Liquid Surface lies.
To Life and Light restor'd, the mourning Fair
Her Plaints continues still, and her Despair;
On Death, and on the *Stygian* Pow'rs, she calls,
'Till fast into the Arms of Sleep she falls.
She now forgets her Sorrow, and her Pains,
Now rest her weary Limbs, and Fancy reigns.
Sweet Images, a various Scene, arise,
To these sweet Thoughts succeed, and sweeter Joys.

CALLIPÆDIÆ.

For Fancy to the sleeping Nymph appears,
A Nymph her self, and various Shapes she wears.
Her Figure now is huge, and now 'tis small,
Now fair, and now deform'd, now short, now tall.
This Species now, and now she that assumes,
With Lights environ'd now, and now with Glooms.
No Rules confine her in her airy Flight,
But wond'rous are her Works, and great her Might.
When Sleep had on the Nymph her Mantle spread,
A pleasing Form she took, and thus she said,
Cease, lovely *Phyllyra!* to wound thy Eyes
With Weeping, and to rend thy Breast with Sighs.
Thy self the Cause of all thy present Woe,
Since all did from thy working Fancy flow.
For *Saturn*, like a Horse that winch'd and neigh'd,
Thy strong Imagination still survey'd.
And with the foul Idea thus defil'd,
It stamp'd the Brutal Image on the Child.
I, who to Human Minds all Forms present,
And make 'em or on this or that intent,
Have often seen thee all thy Soul employ,
To Meditate the God's detested Joy;
His rugged Limbs, and his impetuous Force,
As thy soft Arms embrac'd the mimick Horse.
To shun his scolding Wife, when in the Wood
A Hairy Back bely'd the Hoary God.

CALLIPÆDIÆ.

Full of his Savage metamorphos'd Shape,
His Fierceness figure, and the fatal Rape.
This Image to thy Womb by Thought convey'd,
A Man and Beast the double *Fœtus* made;
And join'd a Horse's Tail and Human Head.
Had ne'er thy vile Imagination fix'd
On his rude Form, the Birth had ne'er been
    mix'd.
The Beast had never to the Man been join'd,
Hadst thou ne'er bid me Paint him to thy Mind.
But Uncorrupt, had sprung from Seed Divine,
An Off-spring worthy a Celestial Line.
Now let us to thy mournful Soul present
A Scene of coming Joy, and sweet Content.
Just Heav'n has Blessings for the Boy in store,
And to the Skies his future Shame shall soar.
Reject not what I say, as false or vain,
For Idle Dreams I do not always feign.
But Conscious of the Fates, pronounce their Doom,
And mark the Past, the Present, and To come.
When number'd Years the ripen'd Man compleat,
Great tho' thy Grief, thy Joy shall be as great.
In Wisdom he shall mate the Gods, and know
All Nature's Works above, and all below.
She'll nothing from his piercing Search conceal,
But all her Secrets, all her Stores, reveal.

CALLIPÆDIÆ.

To him the starry Worlds shall be disclos'd,
The Earth to him, the Crystal Heav'ns expos'd,
Herbs hidden Virtues he shall find, and tell
What Weeds will poison, and what Plants will heal.
His Shape corrupted with the Bestial Kind,
Shall lose its Vileness in his Godlike Mind.
Fair *Thetis* shall to him her Son resign,
And Great *Achilles* owe his Fame to thine.
The *Phantom* said; and into Air dissolv'd,
While in her Mind the Nymph her Speech revolv'd.
She waking, finds her Pain and Sorrow cease,
Her Body's now, and now her Mind at ease.
Her Rest, her Vision, and her Hopes, impart
Light to her Eyes, and Pleasure to her Heart.
Since by foul Objects filthy Births are made,
And the vile Picture's to the Womb convey'd,
A pregnant Wife will ne'er behold a Whale,
Nor Porpus, nor the Dolphin's Azure Scale.
Nor thee, Oh *Proteus*, will she see; nor you
Tritonian Monsters, while she's Teeming, view;
But let her on the lovely *Nereids* gaze,
And fix her Eyes on ev'ry charming Face.

   Ye Pregnant Wives, whose Wish it is, and Care,
To bring your Issue, and to breed it Fair,
On what you look, on what you think, beware.

CALLIPÆDIÆ.

A Boy your Wish, a beauteous Boy behold,
With Lips a Cherry red, and Locks of Gold;
Like him for whom *Alexis* sigh'd of old.
Or in *Apollo*'s Radiant Youth delight,
And like *Apollo*, shall the Birth be bright.
  If Female Fruit you rather covet, view
A Heav'nly *Venus*, such as *Titian* drew.
Or beauteous *Danae*, when her Virgin Flow'r
By *Jove* was gather'd, in the Golden Show'r.
But if the Beauties of our Age can please,
Fair *Phyllis* view; for she's as Fair as these.
View her as when we first beheld the Dame,
And in each Bosom felt a kindling Flame.
How bright her Bloom, her Vernal Glories shine,
How red her Lips, how Lilly white her Skin?
The Loves in ev'ry Look their Sweets display,
In ev'ry Part a thousand Graces play.
But how inconstant is our Human State,
How chang'd is *Phyllis*, how decay'd of late?
The Pride of Youth she can no longer boast,
The Graces, and the Loves, with Time are lost.
Now Furrows in her Face her Age betray,
And the few Hairs that hide her Head are grey.
Now her black Gums for want of Grinders gape,
And safe are such as did the Conqu'ror 'scape.

CALLIPÆDIÆ.

For now those Eyes, that once created Love,
With a dim Light and dying Lustre move.
We scorn those Fires we cou'd not once endure;
Her Youth was the Disease, her Age the Cure.
So chang'd is *Phyllis*, she's a Spectre grown,
And when she's near, ye Teeming Wives, be gone;
Lest the foul Image, on your Mind imprest,
Defile the Seed with which your Womb is blest.

  Who do's not *Chariclæa*'s Story know,
Her Mother black, yet she as white as Snow;
For when the Royal *Ethiopian* bred
The *Fœtus* in her Womb, from *Negroe* Seed,
Her Eyes, *Andromeda*'s bright Picture Charm'd,
By gazing often, she her Fancy warm'd.
The Seed, affected by each greedy Look,
The fair Impression from her Fancy took.
Thus a white Princess from a *Negro* Queen,
A monst'rous, but a beauteous Birth, was seen.
What Dangers hence, what Fears of Death ensu'd,
For long the Jealous King disown'd his Blood.
The naked *Sages*, with their artless Schemes,
In vain their Figures try'd, and holy Dreams:
'Till wise *Sisimithres*, the Master Priest,
The Cause of the prodigious Off-spring guest;
From Fancy's Pow'r the wond'rous Birth deriv'd;
The King believ'd him, and his Consort liv'd.

CALLIPÆDIÆ.

But since, great Prophet of hot *Meroe*'s Tribe,
Nor how the *Fœtus* did the Form imbibe,
Nor how the Virgin lost her Parent Hue,
Thou didst not say——let me the Search pursue;
Let me, by diligent Inquiry, strive
From the true Cause this Wonder to derive.

For this the *Stag'rites* Rules will not suffice,
On which the Schools have set so high a Price.
A better Light I want, a better Guide,
And shall in *Epicurus* be supply'd.
I'll in his Garden trace the Rise of Things,
The source of Nature's Work, and hidden Springs.
And this more clear in our *Gassendus* see,
None Wiser, none more Learn'd, in this, than He.
None dug so deep into her Latent Store,
None search'd so far, and none discover'd more.

Whate'er in Nature may be said to be,
Whate'er we by the Sense or feel or see,
Thin Atoms in the ambient Air distill,
And all things with a Flux eternal fill.
These are the Images of all things stil'd,
And the whole Space with fluid Bodies fill'd.
About they in Successive Order fly,
And pierce the Pores, but 'scape the searching Eye;
Yet Imperceptible affect the Sight,
Mix with the Rays, and flow around with Light.

CALLIPÆDIÆ.

From thence the Eye no pow'rful Atoms brings,
But what the Image forms with rapid Wings.
  Such as from kind and pleasant Objects rise,
Tickle the Senses, as they fix the Eyes.
Their Figure round, the Roundness gives Delight,
Engage the Soul, as they regale the Sight.
The little Balls are thro' the Pores convey'd,
And thus the Semblance is by Fancy made.
They gain the warm Recesses of the Heart,
And are from thence diffus'd to ev'ry Part.
From thence they to the Womb their Passage make,
And young Conceptions thus their Likeness take.
Fair if the Object, will the Atoms be,
And with their Shape the future Birth agree.
From a foul Figure if the Image flows,
The *Fœtus* foully like the Object grows.
The Soul and Eyes it will at once offend,
And filthy Atoms on the Womb descend.
Like little Darts the lab'ring Mind it stings,
And cruel Hate, and anxious Horror, brings,
When the base Likeness on the Babe imprest,
To light is brought, and breaks the Parents Rest.
For if the Seed conceiv'd a Shape assumes,
Wove with those particles in Nature's Looms,
In her first Work the Semblance she receives,
And the vile Image on the Infant leaves.

CALLIPÆDIÆ.

Nor wonder why the *Fœtus* shou'd assume
The Likeness sooner in the Latent Womb,
Than she, who with fix'd Eyes the Object views,
No Look, the Figure, Time has bound, can loose.
But as the tender Fruit which loads the Boughs,
Still suffers most when stormy *Eurus* blows,
Most shatter'd by the rattling Tempest's shock,
Whose Fury scarce affects the Parent stock:
Thus oft, while in the Cell the Infant lyes,
Some Image, present to the Mother's Eyes,
Directs her Forming Mind, and oft destroys
Her Likeness, or the Father's, in the Boy's.
Nature do's there her wond'rous Work begin,
With the fine Parts of Human Frames within;
The Outward then she forms, and spreads the
    Skin.
Both these, and those, by flowing Blood are made,
And her chief Art is to adorn the Head.
Then nothing in your minds revolve, ye Wives,
That an ill Image to a *Fœtus* gives.
On nothing Shocking look, or that may spoil
The beauteous Work, or what you bear, defile.
Nor is't enough, that you the Mind delight
With Objects grateful to the greedy Sight;
From Motions violent, ye Pregnant Fair,
Refrain betimes; the frequent Dance forbear.

CALLIPÆDIÆ.

Not only when the Seed the Tiller Sows
The Frisk forego, but when the Harvest grows.
By tender Strings the growing *Fœtus* sticks,
Both when you feed the Grain, and when you mix.
Abortions, cruel Mothers, hence arise,
Or crooked Births, which you'll, when Born, despise.
If the soft Limbs with furious Leaps you shake,
You'll bend the little Plant, and often break.
Thus, by rude Dances, *Coo* spoilt the Birth,
And brought of old a new Conception forth.
She broke the Stems which did the *Fœtus* bind,
And from the Stock the Jelly Mass disjoin'd.
When an eighth Moon shall in the Skies advance,
Avoid ev'n then, ye Wives, the nimble Dance;
Lest rashly you the rip'ning Birth destroy,
And break the Bands which bound the quicken'd Boy.
A racking Labour shall chastize your Crime,
And a red Flood prevent the promis'd Time.
Mad is that Matron who to Balls resorts,
And, Teeming, gives a Loose to rampant Sports.
But though I interdict the Dance, from hence
She shou'd not draw a dang'rous Consequence;
Or think, that I of too much Ease approve:
You must not leap, and therefore will not move.
The Mean you shou'd observe between 'em both,
Nor too much Action use, nor too much Sloth.

CALLIPÆDIÆ.

The Mean is ever best; an idle Life
Is always hurtful to a Pregnant Wife.
Humours, by Laziness contracted, fill
The Body, and the Native Vigour kill.
Nor can the sacred forming Virtue work,
While in the Blood those Pois'nous Juices lurk.
Its Force it can't exert, nor Strength, nor Grace
Infuse into the Child, whose injur'd Race
Shall long lament the Mother's fatal Ease.
Light Exercise refreshes, off it throws
The Parts which are too heavy and too gross;
It feeds and quickens Nature's latent Fire,
And helps th' Imprison'd Infant to perspire.
Thus when he breaks his Passage from the
    Womb,
The livelier he'll to Light, the stronger come.
What Labour for the Fair shall we devise,
When Teeming, what refreshing Exercise?
Shall we the Chariot recommend, or Chair,
To Ease her Limbs, and suck the purer Air?
The Circle shall she haunt, where artful Rows
Of lofty Elms extend their shady Boughs;
Where the *Seine* waters, with his Chrystal Tides,
The Shores, and thro' *Parisian* Meadows glides?
How will her Heart with secret Pleasure spring,
To see the Coaches whirl around the Ring?

CALLIPÆDIÆ.

The noble Youth to view, the lovely Maid,
Whose Eyes illuminate the crowded Shade?
A Youth see there, in Manhood's radiant Dawn,
Like *Phœbus* in his Golden Chariot drawn.
How white the Locks that hide his Iv'ry Neck,
And flow in Silver Curls adown his Back?
How rich his Dress? How gay his spreading Plume,
And how the Beauties blush when e'er they see him come?
When in his shining Orb he makes his way,
And gilds the Circle like another Day.
See in the farther Round a Virgin Fair,
And mark the Silken Tresses of her Hair.
See how her budding Paps begin to rise,
What Fires are kindled by her sparkling Eyes.
Her the glad Youth with Joy and Wonder view,
Him the gay Nymphs with wishing Eyes pursue.
Her he adores, and as she passes by,
Salutes her lowly with a Look and Sigh,
And smiling on his Love, her Eyes reply.
A grateful Glance the grateful Lover Charms,
And ev'ry Smile a thousand Hearts alarms.
These pleasant Sights the Pregnant Lady please,
And joyous Thoughts her working Fancy seize.
But now the Beauties to retire begin,
The Shade grows empty, and the Circle thin.

CALLIPÆDIÆ.

The Charioteers now lash their foaming Steeds,
And rashly each to gain the Portal speeds.
Here one to get before another strives,
And with loose Reins a third before 'em drives.
Hence Noise, Confusion hence, and broken Wheels,
And often Chance th' inverted Fair reveals.
The Chariot over-turn'd, to vulgar Eyes
Expos'd, the Cast uncover'd Beauty lyes.
Thus oft, alas! she wounds her lovely Face,
And cuts her Forehead with the broken Glass.
Or dislocates her Limbs; ye Teeming Fair,
This vain Contention to be first, forbear.
Last from the Circle let your Chariot come,
And with a gentle Wheel convey you home.
For if you shou'd not over-turn; the Fear
Of falling, while the Latent Fruit you bear,
Abortions may produce, and frozen Blood,
Suppress the flowing of the vital Flood,
And choak the living Heat; nor act its Part,
Or in the burthen'd Womb, or beating Heart.
Such Mischiefs to escape, avoid the Ring,
And mark the Beauties of the painted Spring.
Tread on the Greens, and crop the blowing Flow'rs,
And ease your weary'd Limbs in fragrant Bow'rs.

CALLIPÆDIÆ.

Walk where the feather'd Quires their Vespers sing,
And *Zephirs* fan you with a balmy Wing;
If a fair Boy you'd to the Father bring.
But when the Sun forsakes the Winter Skies,
And hoary Frosts come on, and Snow, and Ice;
When blasted are the Fields, the Forests bare,
What Health, what Pleasure can you hope in Air?
In your warm Sheets, from Cold defended, lye;
Avoid the Rigours of th' Inclement Sky;
And wisely from Outrageous *Boreas* fly.
I warn, to keep within, the Pregnant Spouse,
And all the Winter Moons to love the House.
Shut out the furious Winds and freezing Air,
A lovely and a lusty Boy to bear.
Yet when the North with Rage abated blows,
And a bright Sun with Golden Glories glows;
When fair the Face of Heav'n, and mild the Sky,
Don't on your Couch or lazy Pillow lye.
A friendly Visit make, but go not far,
And with the Neighb'ring Wives divert your Care.
Laugh, Jest, be Joyous, and with harmless Mirth
Relieve the Labours of the growing Birth.

Nor must I here forget a higher Care,
And more incumbent on the Teeming Fair.
Oft to the Temple let the Pregnant Spouse
Repair, and pay to Heav'n her grateful Vows

CALLIPÆDIÆ.

He gives her to Conceive. The Genial Pow'r
Is his, and his the happy Parent Hour.
Oft let her bend before his sacred Shrine,
That he to Virtuous Ways her Off-spring wou'd
    encline.
His Pious Life shall then his Age adorn,
And for a Heav'nly Birth the Child be born.
  These Laws she from Conception must obey,
'Till the ripe *Fœtus* breaks its dang'rous way,
Thro' the dark Dungeon of the Womb, to Day.
And now the Moons begin the Mother's Throws,
Now quick and strong her grinding Labour grows.
The Child's impatient of the promis'd Light,
And struggles thro' the Womb, with all its Might.
But let not his Impatience hurt his Form,
And carefully preserve the Babe from Harm.
A thousand Ills a careless Birth attend,
For now like Wax his pliant Limbs will bend.
If downward with his Feet he strives to come,
Or spreads 'em when he'd leave the lab'ring Womb;
If either Arm he offers to the Neck,
The skilful Midwife gently thrusts it back.
If forward with its Haunch it comes, or Sides,
She mends the Motion, and his Passage guides.
The Head should first appear, the Body next,
Least pain'd is then the Birth, and least perplex'd.

CALLIPÆDIÆ.

Most apt for Passage in this way it lies,
And the first Motion turns it tow'rds the Skies.
Alone, a happy Labour will not do,
The Nurse must in her turn the Work pursue.
A Cradle for the weary Boy prepar'd,
He's swath'd, but see the Swathe be not too hard.
Oft from the Nurses Negligence arise
Hump-backs, and Bandy-leggs, or crooked Thighs.
And if in careless Folds the Babe you wrap,
You'll bend the Figure, and distort its Shape.

As Infants are to many Ills expos'd,
So many remedies has Art disclos'd,
The Native Beauty of the Child to save,
And ev'n improve the Grace that Nature gave.
First then, the Floods that did the *Fœtus* feed
Foul Pustles in the New-born Infant breed.
Prevent the venom'd Sores by timely Art,
And drive the Poison from th' Infected Part.
Most be it to defend the Face your Care,
Lest the cur'd Ulcer leave a gaping Scar.
What Spoil, alas! has this Distemper made?
How low it many a lovely Look has laid?
What Lillies has it kill'd, what Roses chang'd,
What Loves destroy'd, what slighted Youth reveng'd?

When *Galatæa*, in her Virgin Bloom,
Did o'er the Swains a Tyrant Sway assume,

CALLIPÆDIÆ.

She like a Goddess shone, 'till this Disease
Destroy'd her Charms, and gave the Shepherds ease.
In vain she o'er her vanish'd Graces grieves,
What Prints this Ill, what horrid Chasms it leaves.
Amintas, once the Glory of the Plain,
The only lov'd, and only envy'd Swain;
For whom a thousand *Sylvan* Beauties sigh'd,
By this Disease was punish'd for his Pride.
The Marks it left unloos'd the Lovers Chains,
And he's now number'd with the common Swains.
What Med'cines will Relieve, and what will Cure,
A Sickness that's as fatal as impure,
Who dares pronounce on the *Pierian* Hill?
The Secret's left to *Æsculapian* Skill.
And who, that ever read thy Verse Divine,
Thou Great St. *Marthe*, will e'er be pleas'd with mine?
What thou hast Sung shall I presume to Sing?
Who'll dip the Stream, when they're so near the Spring?
All Infant's Plagues they'll from thy Lessons know,
And what the Cure, and whence the Causes flow.
Thy wise Instructions let 'em wisely weigh,
Oft read thy Rules, and what they read, obey.

CALLIPÆDIÆ.

All *Helicon* thy sacred Science drains,
And *Pindus* now a barren Hill remains.
For thee, the *Delphick* God exhausts his Store,
And we can nothing in thy Art explore.
  We'll here awhile the Muses Labours end,
And from our *Pegasæan* Flights descend.
Pleas'd with the painful progress we have made,
Awhile we'll rest beneath the pleasant Shade.
If *Phœbus* shou'd again inspire the Muse,
Perhaps she may a nobler Subject chuse.
As, for the Body, now she Imps her Wings,
She for the Mind perhaps may Tune her Strings.
They both shou'd be alike the Parents Care,
Pure be the Manners, as the Members fair.
What without Virtue is a beauteous Form,
In Strength what Merit, and in Grace what Charm?
And if the Soul is blind with Error, who
A lovely Body can with Pleasure view?
But who wou'd Human Things with Heav'nly join,
Or blend our Earthy Foggs with Air Divine?
Our Iron Age so far from Virtue swerves,
This Task from us, this Toil it scarce deserves.
The Love of Virtue's now, alas! defac'd,
And where's the Man that covets to be Chast?
Honour's an empty Notion, or a Jest,
And Peace despis'd, and Piety opprest.

CALLIPÆDIÆ.

The *French* of Foreign Ways are fond of late,
And War Eternal grieves the *Celtick* State.
　Ye Pow'rs who o'er the *Gallick* World preside,
In better Paths the wand'ring Nation guide.
The Glory of th' *Hectorean* Race sustain,
Let our Rage cease, and Peace assume her Reign.
The Arts will Flourish, when you sheath the Sword,
And to the Bards, the Bays shall be restor'd.

CALLIPÆDIÆ.

BOOK IV.

WHAT barb'rous Sloth my sluggish Soul has seiz'd,
And by what Lazy Pow'r am I possest?
Will *Phœbus* ne'er again the Muse inspire,
And ever will she leave Unstrung her Lyre?
Fair Faces and fine Limbs have try'd her Streins,
But the chief Part that crowns our Work remains.
Man's inward Grace, the Beauty of the Mind,
And Virtue's sacred Charms, are still behind.
Thou Goddess, Born of *Jove*'s Immortal Brain,
Who o'er the Chast unpeopled World dost reign;
Thou Queen of Sciences, Assist my Song,
To thee the Virtues, thee the Arts belong.
Inform the Muse, *Minerva*, for 'tis thine
To guide the Bard, who speaks of Things Divine.

CALLIPÆDIÆ.

Pure Manners who wou'd teach, and how to form
The Mind, must with thy Fire his Fancy warm.
No flame Profane shall *Cytherea* join,
She ne'er shou'd mingle her foul Torch with thine,
Our Subject's spotless, and the Theam divine.

When a Man's Form *Prometheus* made of Earth,
And gave, with Heav'nly Fire, that Form a Birth;
The Race, offended with the Partial Skies,
Begins their rude Beginnings to despise.
Bright in the Image of his Maker born,
The Mortal on his Fortune looks with Scorn.
His base Original he proudly hates,
The Gods he curses, and the guiltless Fates;
That Naked from his Mother's Womb he's thrown;
And, of all Births, he most abhors his own.

What profits me the Flame my Sire might steal,
Th' Etherial Vigour in my Breast I feel?
What profits me my Godlike Mind, he cries,
A Soul aspiring to its native Skies?
What's the poor Life the Gods are pleas'd to grant,
If they have doom'd me to Eternal Want?
What Cov'ring but the Sky, what Bed but Earth,
Had Nature to receive me at my Birth?
Ign'rant, and Infants, by our cries we shew,
As soon as we are Born, that 'tis to Woe.

CALLIPÆDIÆ.

Tho' on the dirty Ground he looks, the Beast
With Strength, as well as Life, betimes is blest.
The Forest Herd defend themselves from Harms,
With Horns, with Teeth, and Hoofs, their native
    Arms.
The Fish with Scales, the Feather'd World with
    Wings,
With Claws and Beeks, the Serpent Fry with Stings.
Nature provides for all the Savage Kind,
And a full Pap in ev'ry Field they find.
A Step-mother to me. I'm forc'd to get
My Bread by Toil, and for my Food to sweat.
The Splendor of the Mind, and boasted Light,
Long lies in Darkness, and in Infant Night;
E'er Wisdom is by dear Experience bought,
Or sooner by a surly Master taught.
To a young Mind, how hard his Rules appear,
How tedious are his Lessons, how severe?
While in the search of Honour, Fame and Truth,
Or of the gen'rous Arts, he guides his Youth.
The rapid Passions while he strives to Rule,
His Lust to Conquer, and his rage to Cool.
Thus deal by Human Race the cruel Fates,
Such Woe on Man, tho' most unworthy, waits.
On the lewd Theam the daring Wretch enlarg'd,
And the Just Gods with foul Injustice charg'd.

CALLIPÆDIÆ.

Who dares with Impious Taunts insult the Skies?
Dost thou, oh Man, thy Maker's Works despise?
Thou to whose Rule he does this World decree,
And bids the whole Creation bend to Thee,
The Joy, the Beauty of it, Thou! Thy Soul
Can all things, if it would it self, controul.
Life is indeed in tender Infants weak,
And brittle is the Frame, and apt to break.
Helpless and naked; but the Mother's Care
Not long neglects the Babe, or leaves it bare.
Strong as it grows, its inward Light extends,
And Time due Vigour to its Knowledge lends.
By Reason, how to Judge aright, he learns,
And what is hurtful, what is good, discerns.
His Wants he knows, and what his Wants supplies,
The Fair he courts by this, the Foul he flies.
By this are Palaces Foundations laid,
Castles are built, and wholesome Laws are made.
By this he far the dreadful Ocean ploughs,
The Air by this, the Starry Heav'ns he knows.
True; By the Body oft the Mind's deprest,
On Earth it oft wou'd with the Body rest.
But when it spreads its Wings aloft it flies,
And reaches in its Flight its Kindred Skies.
With Pious Flames, Etherial Heat, it burns,
And joyous to its Native Heav'n returns.

CALLIPÆDIÆ.

Nor arduous is the Task, when Human Light,
By Grace assisted, gains the glorious Height.
Down on the subject World it looks with Scorn,
Above her Momentary Trifles born.
The sacred Work must be by Art begun,
And Precepts help the Paths of Vice to shun.
The Rule is safe, the Shelves and Sands it shews,
And the Mind stronger by Instruction grows.
Sometimes, tho' rare, the Father's Seed, we own,
In Soul and Body may affect the Son.
If happy be the Skies, the beauteous Race
The Likeness may preserve in Mind and Face.
But oft it fails, and loosly if you breed
Your Off-spring, what avails the gen'rous Seed?
'Tis all by Education lost, the Child
Degen'rates, and the best Beginning's spoil'd.
We never can enough those Parents blame,
Who, careless of a Mother's sacred name,
To Ign'rant Nurses their poor Infants trust;
To such, as neither will nor can be Just.
Oft at a Venal Pap they suck their Bane,
And in their Blood the Latent Plague retain.
But of those Evils not to speak, which flow
From the first Draughts, and with the Body grow;
The Mind's affected by corrupted Juice,
If bad the Milk, the Manners may be loose.

CALLIPÆDIÆ.

Who knows not that a Whore's malignant Pap
Corrupts the Infant, in her wanton Lap:
With Lust and impious Fires it fills his Breast,
And seldom is the Child, so suckled, Chast.
Thou *Romulus*, who in thy Brother's Blood
Deep dip'st, and for thy Rage Commenc'dst a God;
Who by rude Force the *Sabine* Nymph embrac'dst,
Who spoil'dst the *Latian* World, and liv'dst by
    Waste;
To Blood what urg'd thee, to the Spoil and Rape,
But the Wolf's Milk, and horrid Foster Pap?
If Chast the Nurse's Milk, and Manners; hear,
Ye Fathers, what is next a Parent's Care.
In Wisdom's Ways your hopeful Sons to Breed,
And by what Rule you ought their Youth to lead.
For tho' the Boy, unwilling to be Wise,
To study Virtue with Regret applies;
'Tis learnt, like other things, by Exercise.
And thus th' *Athenian* Sage of old aspir'd
To Wisdom, thus her Gifts, her Grace acquir'd.
Nature averse, incessantly he toil'd,
'Till the bright Goddess on his Labours smil'd;
'Till, obstinate to win, he won the Prize,
And by the *Delphick* God was nam'd the Wise.
Not all the Rules to form, the Manners fit,
Not all to write I mean that may be writ.

CALLIPÆDIÆ

But the chief Precepts that the Muse can reach,
And apt for such as Learn, or such as Teach
To bend their tender Minds by sound Advice,
And turn 'em to the Ways, where walk the Wise.

First, e'er the Infant's little Tongue can break
Its Bonds, and while it wants the Pow'r to speak,
With pleasant Food to feed it be thy Care,
And other Helps, that then are useless, spare.
In Beauty and in Strength 'twill grow, and Size,
If stir'd and us'd to gentle Exercise.
The Mind's asleep, and can't as yet display
Its Native Light; for, like the rising Day,
Weak are its Infant Dawn, and Morning Ray.
But as to Noon its spreading Glories rise,
It warms the Worlds around, and gilds the Skies.
As soon as it has learnt a Lisping Speech,
And Human Voice, 'tis thine the rest to Teach.
Inform it of thy Heav'nly Father's Will,
And His dread Laws into its Mind instil.
Its Duty let it know, before the Phrase,
And early let it Lisp its Maker's Praise.
When Lightnings Blast, and Thunders shake the Sphere,
When trembling to thy Lap it flies with Fear,
Tell it 'tis Heav'n's tremendous Voice that roars,
And threatens Vengeance for his slighted Pow'rs.

CALLIPÆDIÆ.

Fear thus prepares it to obey His Law,
And its young Mind is kept in useful Awe.
God may, perhaps, by Reason's Light alone,
If strong the Genius of the Child, be known.
But late it comes, and many rolling Years
Must run their Round, before that Light appears:
Unless betimes the Father's Lessons shew
The forward Son, what he betimes shou'd know.

I pity then their Miserable Fate,
Who never know those Truths, or know too late.
Who ever wand'ring in a Gloomy Way,
To Death in worse than Infant Darkness stray.
Wise in the World, and vers'd in mighty things,
They search the Causes, and the hidden Springs.
Yet Providence's Care they ne'er discern,
Nor how th' Eternal works in all Things learn.
This Knowledge must be taught, 'tis not acquir'd
By Guess, and rarely by the God Inspir'd.

Nor will it be enough, to teach the Boy
The boundless Pow'r of him who Rules on high.
To breed him in his Worship, and his Fear,
So guide him, if he will thy Lessons hear,
That he this sacred Maxim may pursue,
To do himself what he'd have others do.
With grateful Heart his Parents to revere,
Why shou'd I name? The Duty is so clear.

CALLIPÆDIÆ.

Or why his Kindred to respect, or Age,
Or why the Just, the Noble, and the Sage?
The Magistrate to honour, why? For none
In this will leave untaught the Docile Son.
When by Degrees his mental Vigour grows,
Let him no Time to form his Studies lose,
But early put him to the forming Muse.
His Service now th' *Aonian* Sisters claim,
When soft his Brain, and like his Waxen Frame.
Whate'er his Mind receives, the Impression's strong,
And Art as well as Love affects the Young.
Whom will the Mother of the Nine inspire?
That Courts her with an old and languid Fire.
From *Grecian* first, and from the *Latian* Store,
His Mind let him enrich with ancient Ore.
The Names of things, the things themselves
    acquire,
To know, what known, he'll ne'er enough admire
With the dead Languages when he has done,
The Living let him Learn, and first his own:
Study the Beauties of the *Celtick* Tongue,
Where best 'tis written, or where best 'tis Sung.
Th' *Iberian*, tho' a Pompous Phrase, affords
Some Profit in its strong and sounding Words.
These let him Master with assiduous Toil,
His Judgment thus Improve, and thus his Style.

CALLIPÆDIÆ.

Historick Truths, and Heroes deathless Deeds,
As Fame records, the painful Student reads.
But Stories by a Mimick Fancy feign'd
Of Kings and Men, who never Liv'd nor Reign'd;
The vain Romance, in Vogue with Fools, he'll hate,
And all the Visions that have swarm'd of late.
He'll learn to treat these worthless Toys as Lies,
And ev'ry thing that is not true, despise.
But most he loves the Poets sacred Lay,
And with the Chast *Pierian* Nymphs to play.
To him their Fury do's Divine appear,
Their Musick such as Gods might deign to hear.
To Virtue thus with Pleasure he's inclin'd,
And charms his Sense when he informs his Mind.
But when his Years encrease, his Heat within,
And Strength without, the trying State begin.
Strong grow his Passions, and with prudent haste,
Direct his Reason, then to grow as fast.
His boyling Blood can scarce its Rage restrain,
And hard it is for Youth to hold the Rein.
Thick Tempests rise around his crowded Soul,
And furious Waves o'er gentle Reason roul.
'Till Wisdom penetrates the Starless Night,
Restores the Calm, and spreads her Beamy Light.
  Go on brave Youth, the Paths of Virtue tread,
And ben't by Error's devious Tract mis-led.

CALLIPÆDIÆ.

'Till free from Filth, and Spotless is thy Mind,
'Till pure thy Life, and of th' Etherial Kind.
For this we must believe, when e'er we die,
We sink to *Styx*, or to *Olympus* fly.
Two Worlds Just Heav'n for our Reward prepares,
Hell for the Wicked, for the Good the Stars.
Our highest Wisdom this, and our Desire,
The proudest Thought of Man can soar no high'r,
Than God, his Maker, and himself to know;
Above to look, and scorn the Things below.
And since the Quire of Virtues are controul'd
By Reason, and by th' Understanding rul'd:
Since to sound Manners Knowledge leads thee, strive
High as thou canst in Science to arrive.
Tho' Darkness thickens, and Confusion crowds
Around thee, this will scatter all the Clouds.
But Knowledge in some narrow Minds declines,
And with weak Rays Celestial Science shines:
The Love of Truth, and of the gen'rous Arts,
Ne'er works its way, or in their Heads or Hearts.
This Mischief springs from the Mechanick Frame;
When a thick Vapour choaks the Lambent Flame.
Or, poor in Light, they stupidly behold
Whate'er they see, and hear whate'er they're told.
If or from this or that it flows, do thou,
As Fate commands, the Fields of Knowledge plough,

CALLIPÆDIÆ.

And cultivate thy Mind; but ben't so vain,
To fancy thou canst Godlike Knowledge gain;
As far as thou may'st Nature's Depths explore,
Still Inexhaustible thou find'st the Store.
Thee let the Order she observes suffice,
What Laws controul our Earth, and what the Skies.
Mark how a thousand Starry Orbs on high,
Around the Void with equal Motion fly.
Mark how the Huge Machine one Order keeps,
And how the Sun th' Etherial Champian Sweeps;
Both Earth and Air with Genial Heat he warms,
Gives ev'ry Grace and ev'ry Beauty Forms.
Whether around the Lazy Globe he rolls,
Or Earth is whirl'd about him on her Poles,
God is the Mover; God the living Soul,
That made, that acts, and animates the whole.
Hence with thy Atoms, *Epicurus*, Hence;
Was all this wond'rous Frame the Sport of Chance?
Of Solids, they, 'tis true, the Matter make,
Can Matter from its self its Figure take?
Can the bright Order in the World we see,
The blind Effect of wanton Fortune be?
Did jumbling Atoms form the various kind
Of Beings? or did one Almighty Mind?
Guess what you will, you must at last resort
To a first Cause, and not to Chance's Sport.

CALLIPÆDIÆ.

This Cause is God, and how like God shou'd we,
If we cou'd know his secret Councils, be?
If we cou'd trace the Rise of Things, how bright,
How like his own, wou'd shine our borrow'd Light?
Discording Elements how Nature blends,
Why Upwards one, another Downwards tends;
Of Stones, and Plants, the sev'ral kinds to know,
And how in Earth's deep Womb hard Metals grow.
How wou'd it raise our Thoughts, if Grain and Trees,
If Winds, or Ebbing Tides, and flowing Seas,
The Forest Herds, the Fields, the Genial Fires,
We knew, the Scaly Fish, and Feather'd Quires;
And if we in Perfection cou'd rehearse,
The various Wonders of the Universe?
But most our Knowledge shou'd to Man incline,
The wond'rous Fabrick of his Form Divine.
To him, who o'er the vast Creation Reigns,
And his wide Sway by Reason's Rules maintains.
What is there scatter'd in th' Expanded Round,
But in Man's Nature may alone be found?
Do's not his Front resemble that of *Jove*,
When o'er the Gods he sits enthron'd above;
Wing'd Quires attending at his awful Nod,
To waft the Orders of the dreadful God?
Thus in the Head of Man the Soul presides,
Informs the Body, and the Members guides.

CALLIPÆDIÆ.

The Spirits there Unite, and there they shed
Th' Etherial Light that o'er his Frame they spread.
Who knows not that the Heart's the Sov'reign Seat
Of Life, that there the Vital Fountains meet,
And feed and fill the whole with living Heat.
But oft, as from the Sun hot Rays are hurl'd,
That blast the Air, and burn the Subject World;
So in the Heart when boiling Choller reigns,
And furious Lust enflames the fev'rish Veins;
What parching Heat destroys the Human Frame?
And nothing can or quench or check the Flame.

What shou'd I of the Paunch's Burthen tell,
When in its Deep collected Humours swell?
As the Earth's Filth's contracted in the Sea,
And never is it thence from Vapour free;
Thus Foggs and *Flatus* from the Belly rise,
And to the Head and Breast the Mischief flies:
From whence, in Perspiration thro' the Pores,
It drops a kindly Dew like falling Show'rs.
Or rather as thick Clouds and Mists impure,
The Sun's full Beams or Rosie Dawn obscure.
So Humours in the foul *Abdomen* lie,
Which soon to Vapours turn, and mount on high.

CALLIPÆDIÆ.

Chaos and Night they spread, no chearful Ray
The Soul enlightens, 'till returning Day
Breaks thro' the horrid Gloom its Golden way.
But mostly it concerns a Human Mind,
Her self to know, and her Ætherial Kind.
For nothing is more Precious; since her State
To Death's superior, and secure from Fate.
Eternal, Immaterial, and when free
From Guilt, there's nothing so like God as she.
And tho' in ev'ry Part diffus'd she Lives,
Tho' Life she to the Lump and Motion gives,
Yet from the Mortal Body she's disjoin'd.
The Latent Nature, and abstracted Kind
Of things, she by her Light Innate discerns,
Or by Reflection, what she pleases, learns:
As far at least as Human Light can go,
Clog'd by the Clay that covers it below.
Thus tho' on high th' Omnipotent controuls
The World Immense, and round it ever rolls,
The Motion's his; he guides the hidden Springs.
His, tho' the Times and Turns of Human Things,
Himself to nothing owes his Boundless Might,
And shines Eternal with his proper Light.
When Emulous of Gods, the Mind to know
Her worth begins; is she Content below?

CALLIPÆDIÆ.

Will she of Filth be fond, in Dross confide,
The Joys of Sense, or the Deceit of Pride?
Or rather will she not such Toys despise,
Grow proud of Virtue, and asham'd of Vice?
For if the Virtuous with himself shall dwell,
And Heav'n has doom'd the Vicious Soul to Hell:
Who thinks he's of the blissful State secure,
Whose Wishes are not Chast, nor Manners pure;
Whom Wisdom do's not please, who loves to stray
From the streight Path, and takes the wider Way;
Who do's not Fortune's Smiles and Frowns disdain,
Grief, meager Poverty, Contempt and Pain.
For Worldly Ills agree with Virtue best,
And Wisdom flourishes when she's deprest.

Since thou in Life must various Duties mix,
Thou must not on thyself thy Virtues fix.
Allow thou may'st deserve with Gods to live,
Some Cares thou still must to thy Country give.
To publick Offices apply thy Mind,
And study to be useful to Mankind.
For was not Man a Civil Creature born?
And shou'd not he his Soul with Civil Gifts adorn?

Since with all Men all Studies don't agree,
First what's the Genius of the Student see.
In that Indulge him. If to War he bends
His Mind, or if to Peaceful Arts he tends.

CALLIPÆDIÆ.

War may be Lawful, and the Murd'ring Trade
A Science, not a mean one, now is made;
But shou'd be most the Business of the Young,
When their Blood's warm, their Manly Sinews strong.
Beware lest whilst thou haunt'st the Martial Field,
Thy Morals do not to Corruption yield.
For apt is War a Hopeful Youth to spoil,
And Arms the Purity of Life defile.
From Furious *Ennyo* frighted Virtue flies,
And its mild Spirit Martial Minds despise.
But Christians shou'd not Wars with Pleasure wage,
Nor madly imitate the *Thracian* Rage;
Where the fierce Nations deal in impious Arms,
Insensible of Peace's softer Charms.
They never with fine Arts their Souls refine,
Of *Pallas* never heard, nor of the Nine.
By gentle Studies purge thy cruel Mind,
And let mild *Phœbus* with rude *Mars* be join'd.

By Travel crown the Arts, and learn abroad
The Gen'ral Virtues which the Wise applaud.
To Study Nations I advise betimes,
And various Kingdoms know, and various Climes;
Whatever worthy thy Remarks thou seest,
With Care remember, and forget the rest.
This do, before what course of Life to take,
Thou dost, a vain, a rash Election make.

CALLIPÆDIÆ.

Take from their Manners what for thine is fit;
Each Province has its Ways, each People have their
 Wit.
Thee it becomes, their Customs to observe,
To mark where right they walk, and where they
 swerve.
What Virtue here prevails, and there what Vice,
Whose Politicks are Weak, and whose are Wise.
 Thee first fair *Italy* invites, whose Seas
Defend, with double Dykes, her smiling Peace.
Once Empress of the World, she then cou'd
 boast
A Sway from *Indus* to the *British* Coast;
But now her Pride is sunk, her Pow'r is lost.
Religion is her only Glory now,
And the bright Shrines to which the Nations bow.
Here Lazy Soldiers sleep on rusty Shields,
And a light Spear with Pain the *Latian* wields.
In slavish Sloth they live, their Fathers Fame
They now forget, and *Rome*'s Imperial Name.
What Heroes has the Sacred City giv'n
To Earth of old, and thence what Stars to Heav'n?
Nor is their ancient Virtue quite destroy'd,
By which they Conquer'd, and the World enjoy'd.
What mighty Minds, what bright Examples theirs,
How glorious was their Peace, how great their Wars?

CALLIPÆDIÆ.

The Huge Machine upon its Axis roll'd,
For them and Kings by Consuls were controul'd.
Go tread the famous Paths by *Cæsar* trod,
Where he Commenc'd a King, and *Romulus* a God.
Our * *Julius* brightens now the *Celtick* Sphere,
Rome's second Pride, a new *Ausonian* Star.
In him the *Scipio's* and the *Fabii* shine,
And in one Breast their sev'ral Virtues join.
Not him, the proud *Iberians* bloody Rage
Can awe, when wide and bloody Wars they wage.
Not him, *Tisiphone*, whose Band excites
The *Gaul* to mutual Wounds, and mutual Fights.
Not him, foul Slander hurts with Pois'nous Breath,
Nor meagre Envy wounds with venom'd Teeth.
Their latent Snares he scorns, their open Spite;
In vain they threaten him, in vain they bite.
Where in th' *Ausonian* Nations you may find,
Their ancient Courage, and their Strength declin'd.
The wily Ways of subtle Minds you meet,
Soft are their Manners, and their Language sweet.
Their flowing Eloquence, and flatt'ring Air,
Are fine, if false, and if deceitful, fair.
For ev'ry Art th' *Italians* are renown'd,
And sweet's their science when 'tis not profound.

---

* *Mazarine.*

CALLIPÆDIÆ.

No Toil he spares, who covets to be Wise,
But runs with Patience 'till he wins the Prize.
No distant Hopes discourage him, no Pains,
No Frown of Fortune; what he wants he gains.
Frugal and Provident, Expence he flies,
And tho' he will not waste his Wealth, enjoys.
For Industry and Wit, th' *Italian* Name
Is spread, and for a happy Muse, by Fame.

 Thy Travels if by *Spain* thou dost pursue,
A haughty Nation, and a fierce, thou'lt view;
Who wou'd two Worlds by wicked War subdue:
Whose wild Ambition, and their Lust of Sway
Ne'er rest, and who on all Mankind wou'd prey.
What Perils have they undergone, what Toil,
What Empires ruin'd, by their greedy Spoil?
What daring Deeds their cruel Pride inspires?
And nothing can content their mad Desires.
To Conquest they thro' Winds and Tempests fly,
Thro' Seas unknown, and to another Sky.
Nor Thirst, nor Hunger, can their Rage retain,
So fond are they of an unbounded Reign,
But tho' this blind Desire of boundless Sway
Prevents; no Host like these their Heads obey.
With such dread awe, no Military Bands
Submit to their Superior's harsh Commands.

CALLIPÆDIÆ.

Their Courage constant, and their Martial Flame
Still Blazes, and with them's no Vice like Shame.
The Glebe neglected, and such rural Cares,
Unprun'd they leave the Vine, and seek the Wars:
Each arms, and to the Spade the Spear prefers.
A Lordly Spirit burns in ev'ry Breast,
And gladly they for Rule renounce their Rest.
In Arms not only, but in Council Great,
Thou'lt many of the chief *Iberians* meet.
Tenacious of their Secrets, close and proud;
Religion they pretend, to cheat the Crowd.
Thus vulgar Minds with Biggot Zeal they fill,
Thus colour their Designs, and cloak when ill.
Thy Ears the *Spaniard* with big Words will stun,
Yet ev'ry Tongue despises, but his own.
With a loud Bounce their tamed Speech is spoke;
And yet how soon the Blaze dissolves in Smoke?

But if the Sun those barren Climes to burn
Thou leav'st, and dost to fruitful *France* return:
The *Pyrenæan* past, thou there wilt find
A Nation temper'd of a various Kind,
And Mild and Fierce, and Rude and Gentle, join'd.
Good Offices, or ill, pass lightly by,
And neither long in their Remembrance lye.
Not forward to Revenge, or to Oblige,
But yet their Swords are not without an Edge.

CALLIPÆDIÆ.

Their Native Levity to Valour yields,
And none more fierce or bold in Fighting Fields.
How oft has mighty *Rome* with Terror shook,
When the brave *Gauls* have like a Torrent broke
Her Fences, and she fear'd the *Gallick* Yoke?
How far have they advanc'd with Conqu'ring Hosts
Beyond, or *Asian* Shoars, or *Lybian* Coasts?
How oft their Arms have in the East been fam'd,
And Nations *Rome* cou'd never tame, have tam'd?
But seldom lasting is their Martial Fire,
In peaceful Intervals the Flames expire.
If ill the Issue, the Beginning fair,
The're balkt, and of a better Fate despair.
Whence do's this Negligence of Glory rise?
Is't that their Heat away in Vapour flies,
Or those whom once they've beaten, they despise?
Or is it that their vain inconstant Mind,
Is still to Novelties too much inclin'd?
That now they're bent, and now averse to War,
And now the Olive, now the Bays prefer.
No Nation like the *French* a Crown adore,
None love their Monarch, none revere him more.
His Pleasure they with Pride obey and fear,
And Majesty is in full Glory here.
His Realms he with Despotick Edicts awes,
Edicts are Statutes, and his Will, the Laws.

CALLIPÆDIÆ.

And shou'd a Boy his Father's Sceptre sway,
The Subject wou'd the same Obedience pay.
What shall I mention of the *Gallick* Court,
Of Foreign Worth, as she's the full Resort?
How kindly she her noble Guests receives,
And when ill Times prevent her, how she grieves.
For *France* to Alien Merit's always kind,
And Favour there, whoe'er deserves it, find.
For Council fit, if apt for Great Affairs,
In Wisdom eminent, or fam'd in Wars.
Whoe'er are thus, will, as they merit, fare,
And Virtue's ne'er reputed Foreign there.
He now who at the Helm her Empire guides,
How well he for her Wants and Wars provides?
The *Roman* Prince with *Latian* Purple drest,
How easie are we in his Rule, how blest?
While singly he with steady Soul sustains
The *Gallick* World, and for her Monarch Reigns.
He like a new *Alcides* spreads her Fame,
And will again the *Spanish Geryon* tame.
Not only civil Manners, free Access,
Not chearful Looks alone, and fine Address,
The *French* distinguish; but the Muse Divine,
And gen'rous Arts with those of Sway they join.
Untouch'd they nothing leave, because abstruse,
And for their Guide the *Attick* Sages chuse.

CALLIPÆDIÆ.

Of these their Eloquence they learn; to Sing
Of the Nine Sisters of th' *Aonian* Spring.
To tune th' *Ausonian* Lyre their Poets teach,
And *Roman* Heights by *Latian* Helps they reach.
Of *Latian* Emulous and *Attick* Strains,
We hear their Musick in the *Celtick* Plains.
And when the tender Air they try, or strong,
They Charm alike, and *Phœbus* owns the Song.

  At *Calais* if you cross the Streight, you'll find
The cruel *English* from the World disjoin'd.
Cruel indeed, with Royal Blood defil'd,
A Rabble, Rash, Untameable, and Wild.
With holy Lunacy they're all possest,
And ev'ry Man's a Prophet, or a Priest.
Humour's with them Religion's only Guide,
And each that fatal Rule pursues with Pride.
Each on his Neighbour wou'd his own impose,
And thence This Sect to That are Mortal Foes.
Hence Wars and Woes, while each his Dreams wou'd spread,
Mis-lead the rest, as he's himself mis-led.
Each by the Sword his Doctrine wou'd defend,
Which each believes he has a right to mend.
To Kings alike Rebellious, and the Skies,
All Ancient Rites and Worship they despise.

CALLIPÆDIÆ.

This Madness to a thousand others leads,
Soon as it springs, a new Opinion spreads.
By ev'ry Sex and Age with Heat espous'd,
'Till tir'd by that, they're by the next abus'd.
In something they're however worthy Praise.
For who have like the *English* plough'd the Seas?
Who verst in Nautick Arts, like them have past
The farthest Limits of the Liquid Wast.
Not *Typhis* more, nor mighty *Jason* knew,
Nor all the boasted *Argo*'s vent'rous Crew.

What shou'd I of the *Belgick* Nations say?
From these divided by a narrow Sea.
Their Manners like the *French*, but that they hate
A Kingly Name, and loath a regal State.
Tenacious of their Liberties, they scorn
To wear the Yoak, to which their Sires were born.

With Pleasure thou'lt the *German* World survey,
Where *Cæsar* still asserts Imperial Sway.
Where the proud Eagle rules the spacious Plains,
And all that's left of *Roman* Pride, remains.
Plain are the People, Faithful here, and Kind.
And fair themselves, they hate a fraudful Mind.
But whether 'tis, that thick and cold the Air,
The Brain is chill'd, a ready Wit is rare.
O whether 'tis that by the Vice of Drink,
They drown their Wit, and lose the Pow'r to think.

CALLIPÆDIÆ.

For here the sparkling Glass goes often round,
And thirsty Feasts, and flowing Bowls abound.
Such drunken Revels are with them no shame,
And *Bacchus* always lights the Social Flame.
When in their Cups their friendly Souls they join,
Use makes it lawful to Indulge with Wine.
As kind, so bold they o'er the Bottle grow,
And Mirth and Friendship in their Bumpers flow.
Thus at the *Bacchanals* the giddy Guests,
In Honour of *Silenus* held their Feasts.
Thus to the Gods their Noisie Hymns they sung,
And the Lewd Temples with their Clamour rung.
But 'tis not here an Universal Vice,
And Part at least of both the Great and Wise,
This vulgar and unmanly Joy despise.
Who more Discov'ries have in Science made,
Who more its Use advanc'd, its Glory spread?
The Lightnings of the War, who do's not know,
And Thunders we to *German* Studies owe.
To them th' Immortal Honours of the Press,
And Learning's second Life, and vast Encrease.
Inur'd to War, unactive Ease they hate,
And the soft Leisures of a Peaceful State.
Lest Ease and Sloth shou'd quench their Martial Fire,
They serve their Neighbours in their Wars for Hire.

CALLIPÆDIÆ.

And rather than in lazy Peace they'll Rust,
Their Quarrels Fight; for his, who pays, is just.
   To *Dane* and *Pole* thou may'st at last proceed,
To the Rude *Russian*, and the Martial *Swede*.
For tender as the Muse, and tho' 'tis rare,
She sometimes dwells beneath the Frozen *Bear*.
But thou, perhaps, so far wou'dst not extend
Thy Toil, nor to such various Climes descend.
Such Lengths thou may'st not be inclin'd to go,
The Nations Manners, and their Arts, to know.
Strength such an Enterprize requires, and Wealth,
A Store of Fortune, and a Stock of Health.
From Sea to Sea to pass, from Shore to Shore,
And diff'rent Tracts, and distant Realms explore.
   But when thou to Maturer Years art grown,
And from far Climes again hast reach'd thy own;
Thy Manners when by Travel thou'st refin'd,
Inform'd thy Judgment, and Improv'd thy Mind;
There fix: Some Civil settled Business chuse,
And don't the Labours of thy Travels lose.
Weigh well what Life will with thy Genius suit,
And of the bought Experience, reap the Fruit.
Whate'er thou didst in Foreign Regions view,
Now fly it, if 'twas bad, if good, pursue.
Avoid their Vices, make their Virtues Thine,
And let their Lights, in Thee united, shine.

CALLIPÆDIÆ.

As when *Hyblæan* Bees the Work contrive,
And meditate the Labours of the Hive.
The Woods they search with an unweary'd Wing,
The Gardens and the Greens, to rob the Spring.
And when the Field's refresh'd with Vernal Show'rs,
They sip the Dew, and suck the blowing Flow'rs.
Sweet *Thyme* for them, and grateful *Cassia* grow,
And *Sav'ry* blooms, and Purple *Vi'lets* blow.
Their Sweets from ev'ry Tree and Herb they take,
And *Honey* of their various Juices make.

While thus thy ripen'd Years in Manhood wear,
Preserve the Stock thou hast acquir'd with Care.
Thy Genuine Gifts by Study still improve;
For great Examples ever greatly move.
The Lives of Heroes at thy Leisure read,
What Captains have perform'd, and Sages said.
What thou by Earth may'st learn, or by the Skies,
And all things proper to inform the Wise.
Nor shou'dst thou Conversation's Helps omit,
Which gives to Virtue Strength, an Edge to Wit.
When Good, the kind Contagion's apt to spread,
And Men to Knowledge are by Friendship led.

We can't too much those cruel Parents blame,
Who think their Rank above a Father's Name.
Who never, careless of their Children, mind
With whom they are in League and Friendship join'd.

But freely let 'em their Associates chuse,
And leave 'em to a flowing Rein, and loose.
Thus grow the Noble Youth in Years and Vice,
Herd like the Rout, and Discipline despise.
What hopes such Breeding will to Virtue lead.
The Harvest will be ever like the Seed.
Thence Riots, Gaming, and lewd Scoffs ensue,
And thence the Wanton and the Wasteful Crew.
Unwary Youth, who walk without a Guide,
To Vice will from the Paths of Virtue slide.
Not only they Ignoble Ways pursue,
They never seek, nor wish to find the True.
They blindly follow, as by Passion led.
And ever liv'd deprav'd as they were bred.

 But nothing more corrupts the Callow Lord,
Than *Parasites* that haunt his crowded Board.
They freely to his Plenteous Table come,
Where Virtue's oft deny'd for want of Room.
How loud the sordid Rout their Voices raise?
The Bottles these, and those the Dishes praise.
This with a sparkling Glass the next defies, ⎫
Around it to his Lordship's Wishes flies, ⎬
And each Extols the Liquor to the Skies. ⎭
Another now to *Cupid*'s soft Delights,
By wanton Talk, his kindling Lust excites.

CALLIPÆDIÆ.

Behold, oh Gen'rous Youth, the Flatt'rer cries,
That lovely Virgin Nymph with longing Eyes;
Can neither Bloom thy Heart, nor Beauty move?
Bless, and be blest; Indulge thy self with Love.
The *Solons* thou, the *Cato's* shou'dst despise,
For he, who to be Happy knows, is wise.
This wicked Speech is follow'd by a worse,
Their Guests are such, and such their vain Discourse.

    This spoken; while to speak I still prepare,
What Heav'nly Voice invades my trembling Ear?
What Light is this, which like the Orient Day,
Breaks fresh, and darts a new, a warmer Ray?
Calliope? 'Tis she, 'tis she, I know,
By her mild Aspect, and her bashful Brow.
Her Step the Goddess, and her Mien confess:
To me, why dost thou thus, oh Nymph, address?
Hast thou on *Pindus* heard my daring Lays,
And thence descend'st to give the *Bard* the Bays?

    Go on, said she; and what the Beauteous Nine
Can give to close thy grateful Song, is Thine.
Go on; again they will thy Breast inspire;
Supply thy Muse, and feed thy wasting Fire.
For Males thou shou'dst not only Precepts find,
And study to adorn the Manly Mind:
The Female claims, as she deserves, thy Care,
And Woman shou'd thy useful Lessons share.

CALLIPÆDIÆ.

Beauty is Hers with ev'ry outward Grace,
And fair shou'd be her Mind, as well as Face.
The Manners proper for her Sex, she'd know,
The proper Graces, which you next shou'd shew.
And to the Muses since the Sex belong,
Since Theirs their Virtues, Theirs shall be the Song.
Nor will I, to inform the Fair, disdain,
But thus in friendly Verse their Arts Explain.

  First Woman's Mind is not so weak in force,
Nor is the Clay of which she's form'd so Course;
But she's for the sublimest Knowledge fit,
For ev'ry thing that Art can do, or Wit.
Who dares an Error so absurd maintain,
That Woman either Courage wants, or Brain?
Why mayn't she Causes and Effects inquire?
To ev'ry thing that Man aspires, aspire?
Or why to Man shou'd Fate the Blessing give,
Yet Woman's Soul of Reason's Light deprive?
Why must the Pow'r of Human Minds, in her
Be broken; and the Foolish be the Fair?
The Righteous Gods cou'd ne'er admit such Wrong.
If *Phœbus* is for Science fam'd, or Song,
Tritonian Pallas, and the Sacred Nine,
Of Song and Science boast, and all his Arts Divine.
How were we Worship'd by a Royal Dame,
In elder Times; Reflect, ye *Gauls*, with shame.

CALLIPÆDIÆ.

With thee, oh Daughter of *Valois*, the Pride,
The Boast, in *Gaul*, the Wit of Woman dy'd.
A gen'ral Sloth has seiz'd the Sex, and now
None covet what the Muses teach, to know.

We hence in Honour of the Nine must fly,
To Climes beneath the *Hyperborean* Sky.
Beneficent the *Goths* great Queen we find
To Learning, to the slighted Sisters kind.
Our Laurels with her Father's Wreaths she joins,
And *Mars* his Empire to the Muse resigns.
Oh wondrous turn of Fate! oh Pow'r Divine,
Here now the Noble Arts conspicuous shine;
Whose barb'rous Nations once their Glories hurl'd
To Dust, and ravag'd all the Learned World.
Now mighty is the Change! the *Heroin*'s Care
Has rais'd their Beamy Heads, and crush'd the War.

If less you to the beauteous Arts encline,
Ye *Celtick* Fair! If you neglect the Nine,
Be Good at least, be Modest and Discreet,
And ne'er your Character nor Sex forget.
When Wool you weave, or turn the whirling Wheel,
With flying Fingers, when you charge the Reel,
Or guide thro' pliant Flax the pointed Steel,
Call oft to Mind the Pious *Sabine* Wives,
And form, by theirs, your chast and painful Lives.

CALLIPÆDIÆ.

Who can endure lewd Manners in the Fair?
A *Lais*, or a *Flora*, who can bear?
Who likes, or wanton Smiles, or tempting Leers;
Or what dishonest in the Sex appears?
Not *Psyche* by such fond Enticements strove
To Charm, and yet she Charm'd the God of Love.
For Virtue and a modest Mien inspire
A fierce, a lawful, and a lasting Fire.

   She said, and into fleeting Air dissolv'd,
While in my Soul her sayings I revolv'd,
Sad and confus'd. Oh Goddess, hadst thou pleas'd
With other Wisdom to inspire my Breast,
How had I listen'd to thy sacred Voice?
And now a nobler Theam had been my Choice.
What Gifts of Royal Minds enrich the Throne,
What Arts of Rule I might from thee have known.
And what Heroick Virtue shou'd adorn
The Souls of such as are for Empire born.
How Subjects shou'd obey what Kings decree;
Majestick Truths, I might have learnt from thee
And to the *Celtick* Monarch, fair and young,
From thy Eternal Oracles have sung.
To him that wears the Crown his Fathers wore;
Him whom the *Gauls* with ardent Zeal adore.
How o'er the Mind his Empire to maintain,
Him now I might have told, and how to Reign.

CALLIPÆDIÆ.

That Prince and People, of thy Rules possest,
May they in him, and he in them be blest.
Perhaps he to the gentle Muse wou'd lend
A gracious Ear, and to her Song attend.
But what Stupidity my Mind has seiz'd,
Why shou'd I fancy he'll with Songs be pleas'd?
Or will the Mild, the Peaceful Muses hear,
With Arms encompast, and the Noise of War?

For now th' *Iberian*, with Imperious Soul,
Of half the World possest, demands the whole.
All *Europe* now he rages to subdue,
And nothing we but Arms and Armies view.
The Harp neglected, on the Willow's hung,
And only now the Hostile Bow is strung.
Farewel, *Calliope!* My sacred Fire
Is quench'd, and I awhile must leave the Lyre.

The Time shall come, nor let the Fates delay
The tardy Hour, but wing its welcome way,
When *Spain* shall have her fill of Blood, and cease
Her Fury, found in vain, and sue for Peace.
The Pious Hero, e'en to these, will shew
His Goodness, and forgive the Suppliant Foe.
Then hush'd shall be the Din of War. The Palm
Shall spread, and to the Storm succeed a Calm.
Ambition shall to rest desire, and Fame
The Triumphs of the Muses then proclaim.

CALLIPÆDIÆ.

Then shall great *Lewis*, Crown'd with Olives, meet
The Tuneful Quire; and here they'll fix their Seat.
He in high Palaces shall place the Nine,
And on the Bards with Royal Favour shine.
How then will Ecchoing Courts resound his Praise,
And gilded Roofs return their Joyous Layes!
  But now the Muses, a detested Toil,
Of Arms can only Sing, of Blood and Spoil.
The cruel Causes and Effects of War,
Here Hostile Fleets, and Fighting Armies there.
Here Cities sackt, and others there in Flames,
And spacious Plains enrich'd with Purple Streams.
Where *Celtick* mingled with *Iberian* Blood,
For twenty Suns have swell'd the guilty Flood.
The Theam alternate Waste can only be,
Alternate Triumph, or by Land or Sea.
But then the *Nine* these Slaughters shall forget,
And all their Charming Airs be soft and sweet.
No Martial Verse shall vex the List'ning Ear,
Nor fill the Head with Noise, the Heart with Fear.
On Peace, *Euterpe* shall her Notes employ;
The Food of Pleasure, and the Soul of Joy.
Then *Ceres*, fair and free, the fruitful Field
Shall bless, and ev'ry Tree a Treasure yield.
Then swelling Clusters shall the Vineyard load,
And the Fat flow with the fermenting God.

CALLIPÆDIÆ.

Then the glad Youth our grateful Arts shall try,
And clasp their Beauteous Brides with honest Joy.
Hymen shall often fill the Lover's Arms,
And Charming Boys preserve their Parents Charms.

  So when against the Gods the Gyants rose,
And *Jove* in Battel met his daring Foes;
When by his Lightning huge *Typhæus* fell,
And Headlong *Cæus* follow'd him to Hell.
When Proud *Enceladus* was blasted hurl'd,
From the bright Verge of yon *Empyrean* World.
Whole Heav'n, to celebrate the Joy, requires
Th' *Aonian* Nymphs to Tune their Golden Lyres.
The sacred Sisters strike the trembling Strings,
And all *Olympus* with loud *I O*'s Rings.
Immortal Quiet to the Skies restor'd,
Ambrosian Dishes spread the Chrystal Board.
Around the sparkling Nectar freely flows,
And glad each Deity and gamesome grows.
Love claps his wanton Wings to crown the Feast,
And ev'ry Goddess by her God's Carest.

[BOOK IV.] 110

CALLIPÆDIÆ.

OR,

AN ART

HOW TO HAVE HANDSOME

CHILDREN:

WRITTEN IN LATIN

BY THE

ABBOT CLAUDE QUILLET.

Now done into English Verse
by several hands.

[Fac-Simile of London Editions of 1708–10.]

PHILADELPHIA:
PRINTED FOR THE
AMERICAN ANTIQUARIAN PUBLISHING COMPANY.
1872.

www.ingramcontent.com/pod-product-compliance
Lightning Source LLC
Chambersburg PA
CBHW030406170426
43202CB00010B/1511